The Sleeping Be

A Pantomime

Norman Robbins

Samuel French - London
New York - Toronto - Hollywood

CHARACTERS

Azuriel, a fairy
Fusspot, the Lord Chamberlain
Tickles, the Court Jester
King Cedric VII of Entertainia
Queen Semolina, his wife
Dame Ammonia Goodbody, the Royal Nurse
Carabosse, a wicked fairy
Shout }
Bawl } two heralds
Princess Aurora
Prince Valiant of Euphoria
Chorus of **Courtiers, Villagers, Royalty, Huntsmen**, etc.
Dancing chorus for **Fairies**, etc.
Junior and Babes chorus for **Insects, Fairies**, etc.

SYNOPSIS OF SCENES

PROLOGUE

Fairyland

ACT I

ACT II

MUSICAL NUMBERS

ACT I

Song 1	Choristers
Song 2	Tickles and the Ladies
Song 3	Aurora and Chorus
Music	Insect Ballet
Song 4	Prince and Princess
Song 5	Tickles and Dame
Song 6	Princess
Song 7	Guests and Dancers

ACT II

Song 8	Villagers
Song 9	Prince
Song 10	Prince
Song 11	Queen and Ensemble
Song 12	Prince and Princess
Song 13	Shout and Bawl
Dance	Huntsmen and Game
Dance	Choristers
Finale	

The choice of songs and dance music is left to the individual director. Please read the notice below most carefully:

A licence issued by Samuel French Ltd to perform this play does NOT include permission to use any copyright music in the performance. The notice printed below on behalf of the Performing Right Society should be carefully read.

AUTHOR'S NOTE

Sleeping Beauty has been written as a direct result of dozens of dramatic societies asking me for a script on the subject. As a professional actor and director, I've appeared in versions of this story, several times, and have never been entirely happy with any of them. Mainly, I suppose, because most scripts have the princess appearing in Act I, and the prince only appearing in Act II, meeting for the first time, just before the Finale. Other versions didn't seem to be true pantomime (as we accept it today) and some were downright awful.

I'm not claiming that my version is superior to any other. It wouldn't be true, and it would be very unfair. What I do say, is that I could live with this version. A quick scan through it will tell you if you could.

Staging should be simple. The script is designed for a tiny school hall or a full sized theatre. Props and costume should cause no problem. Songs I leave to the discretion of the Director or MD, and my only advice is to keep it brisk and bouncy.

The giant snake can easily be changed to a larger dragon etc., should you so wish, and it would be nice if the costumes could reflect the passage of one hundred years. If not, don't worry too much. Audiences will accept discrepancy if they enjoy the rest of the show, and we all know the financial problems involved.

Norman Robbins

For

Rev. Michael J. Burgess
Former professional actor and singer

(With great memories of our crimes against the world of theatre over a period of many years)

Other pantomimes by Norman Robbins

Aladdin
Cinderella
The Grand Old Duke of York
Hickory Dickory Dock
Humpty Dumpty
Rumpelstiltzkin
Sing a Song of Sixpence
Tom, the Piper's Son
The Wonderful Story of Mother Goose

Full-length comedy plays by Norman Robbins

Late Mrs Early
Pull the Other One
Tomb with a View
Wedding of the Year

PROLOGUE

Fairyland

When the CURTAIN *rises, six Fairies are revealed posed in graceful attitudes against a shimmering backdrop of dew-covered roses in various shades, and glittering spider webs. Fairy-like music plays softly and the scene should be lit in pale pastels. There is a flash and Azuriel appears* R, *moving* C *in gentle excitement*

Azuriel   Dear sisters. News from Earth I bring. A joyous proclamation.
The mortal Queen and King we guard, today give celebration.
To them a baby girl is born, and though our tasks are pressing,
We're invited to the palace so that each can give her blessing.

The Fairies all look interested

What say you, sisters? Shall we go? If not, give reason why,
And I, Azuriel, myself, shall take them our reply.

Fairies all agree eagerly

Within the week, that tiny babe will have her christening day
And through all Entertainia shall merriment hold sway . . .
So, quickly. Think of all the gifts a princess could require
To make her life enchanting; to fulfil her heart's desire.
Whilst I return to thank them for their gesture most polite,
And assure them that we'll all be there upon the christening night.

Azuriel waves her wand. There is a flash and an instant Black-out

Everyone exits quickly

ACT I

The great ballroom of Entertainia's royal palace

There is a backcloth of a ballroom interior with cut-out windows. Ornate gold pillars mask L *and* R. *Up* L *is a dais with two steps surrounding it and, on top of this, two thrones, high-backed and topped with the crowns of Entertainia. At the side of the dais* R *is a royal cradle. The whole ballroom is decorated with streamers, balloons, flags, etc.*

The Courtiers stand around admiring the decorations. Servants are scurrying around busily, whilst Chefs and Assistants parade by carrying huge dishes of food for the party. The whole atmosphere should be one of excitement and movement. When the scene begins, everyone is singing and dancing as they go about their business

Song 1 (Choristers)

At the end of the song all exit, with the exception of a few Courtiers. At the same time Fusspot, the Lord Chamberlain, hurries in R. *He carries a rod of office at all times*

Fusspot (*looking about him anxiously*) Tickles? *Tickles?* Where on earth can the man be? (*To the Courtiers*) Has anyone seen Tickles?

Girl We haven't seen him all day, Lord Chamberlain. Perhaps he's up in the East Tower again. Inventing something special for the party tonight.

Fusspot (*annoyed*) He's no *right* to be up in the East Tower. He's a court jester, not an inventor.

Boy But you must admit he's invented some marvellous things, Mr Fusspot. A fish-hook with a camera on it, so you can take pictures of the one that got away.

Girl An alarm clock with only half a bell—for waking up one person when two are sleeping in the same room.

Boy The telephone that *doesn't* ring the minute you step into the bath.

Fusspot Yes, yes, yes. I know all that. But just the same he's no business being up there when there's so much work to be done down here. Look at me. Lord Chamberlain of Entertainia, running around like a common servant. Oh, just wait till I get hold of him.

Girl Well now's your chance. Here he comes now.

Tickles the Court Jester enters. He is dressed in traditional jester's clothing and carries a large slice of bread in his hand

Tickles (*brightly*) Hiya, everybody. Here, look what I've just invented. (*He holds up the slice of bread*) Isn't it smashing?

Fusspot (*peering at it*) Bread? You've invented a slice of *bread*?

Tickles No, no. You've got it all wrong, Fussie. This isn't just a slice of bread. This is a slice of bread with *wires* in it.

Fusspot (*blankly*) Wires? (*Baffled*) But what good is *that*?

Tickles Don't you see? It's for people who haven't got electric toasters. They just have to plug the bread into the socket.

The Courtiers laugh and exit casually

Fusspot (*annoyed*) Oooooh. I'm warning you, Tickles. Any more of these *stupid* inventions and I'll report you to their majesties. From now on I don't want to see another invention of yours inside this palace. Is that understood?

Tickles (*protesting*) But Fussie, we've got to have inventions. Where would the world be without them? After all, if Edison hadn't invented the light bulb, we'd all have to watch television by candlelight.

Fusspot Television? Television? What are you talking about. This is the sixteenth century. Television hasn't been invented yet.

Tickles (*startled*) Hasn't it? (*Eagerly*) That's it, then. That's *it*. My next invention. I can be a millionaire before John Yogi Bear's even born. Yippee. (*He jumps up and down with glee*)

Fusspot (*firmly*) Just a minute. *Just a minute*. What did I tell you not two minutes ago? *No more inventions.*

Tickles (*downcast*) Oh, all right. I promise I won't make anything else.

Fusspot Good. Now what kind of entertainment are you going to provide for the guests this evening?

Tickles Oh, just singing and dancing and telling a few jokes.

Fusspot Is that all? You did that at the last party. Isn't there anything else you can do?

Tickles I can tell fortunes.

Fusspot (*surprised*) Tell fortunes? You?

Tickles Oh, yes, I'm very good at telling fortunes.

Fusspot (*interested*) Oh really? I—er—I didn't know that. I—er—I wonder if you could tell *mine*?

Tickles Nothing to it. Just cross my palm with a five pound note. (*He holds out his hand*)

Fusspot (*startled*) Five pound note?

Tickles Oh, yes. You see I answer two questions for that.

Fusspot I see. Yes. Well, that does make a difference. (*He gets out a five pound note and gives it to Tickles*) Now then, the first thing I'd like to know is . . . (*He blinks*) Just a minute. Isn't five pounds for two questions a bit *expensive*?

Tickles Yes. Now what's your *second* question?

Fusspot (*snatching the note back*) Give that here. (*Indignantly*) How dare you try to swindle me out of my money? (*He puts it away*) How dare you?

Tickles I wasn't doing it for myself. I was doing it to help the king and queen.

Fusspot (*peeved*) Don't be so ridiculous. How can diddling me out of my money help *them*?

Tickles Well, they've got none of their own, have they? They're stony broke.

Fusspot Who told you that?

Tickles Nobody. I worked it out for myself. I saw all the fuss they were making this morning when the baby swallowed a penny.

Fusspot (*wincing*) Oh I don't know why their majesties put up with you. You're the worst jester we've ever had at the palace. No-one laughs at your jokes. You can't do somersaults and you don't even play a musical instrument. (*Sternly*) Now listen to me. I'm off to see if the banqueting hall is ready, and I suggest *you* rack your brains for something to do at the party. Let us down tonight and you'll be out of a job tomorrow. (*He begins to exit down* L) And don't forget. No more inventions.

Fusspot exits

Tickles (*sighing deeply*) Oh, I hate being a jester. I want to do something exciting with my life. Nothing ever happens in Entertainia. (*Directly to the audience*) I ran away with a circus once, but the police caught me and made me bring it back again. (*He thinks*) Now what am I going to do for the party? (*Brightening*) I know. I'll give 'em some poetry. (*Reciting*) Mary had a little watch, she swallowed it one day ... and now she's drinking castor oil to pass the time away. (*He shakes his head*) No that's no use. Oh, if only I could show 'em some of my inventions. I know they'd like that. (*Downcast*) Still, I promised old Fusspot, didn't I! Ooooh, I am fed up. (*He brightens*) Here, I know. *You* can cheer me up, can't you? 'Cos if every time I come on and shout "Hiya, kids", you can shout back "Hiya, Tickles", and that'll make me feel better. Will you do that for me? Will you?

Audience reaction

All right then. We'll have a little practice.

He practises with the audience till satisfied

There I feel better already.

Some of the lady Courtiers hurry on and surround him

Ladies (*delightedly*) Tickles.

Tickles (*nervously*) Oh ... hello, ladies.

1st Girl (*pleading*) Say you'll help us, Tickles. *Please.*

Tickles Help you? How?

2nd Girl There's so many ladies coming to the party, we're sure there won't be enough men to go round.

3rd Girl So we were wondering ...

4th Girl If we could persuade you ...

5th Girl To dance at least *one* dance ...

6th Girl With each and every one of us.

All Please. (*They flutter their eyelashes at him, smiling and flirting*)

Tickles (*going weak at the knees*) Oooooooh, I wish you wouldn't do that. I'm coming over all unnecessary. (*Deciding*) All right then. I'll do it on one condition.

1st Girl What's that?

Tickles While I'm dancing with one of *you* the others will keep Dame Goodbody out of the way. You know how bad tempered she gets when she sees me with another woman. The last time she saw me talking to the kitchen maid, she went mad. Said she wouldn't speak to me for a week. (*He bursts into tears*)

2nd Girl (*comforting him*) There, there. You don't have to cry.

Tickles Yes, I do. The week's up today.

3rd Girl Well you don't have to worry. As soon as the christening's over, she'll be taking the baby back to the nursery and we won't see her again all night.

Tickles (*brightening*) Hey, you're right. Well in that case, ladies, I'm all yours.

Ladies Hooray.

Song 2 (Tickles and the Ladies)

At the end of the song, all dance off merrily down L *and as they do so, King Cedric VII enters up* R, *looking glum. He is followed by a radiant Queen Semolina. They move* C

Queen (*happily*) Oh, Cedric, isn't it exciting? The biggest party ever held in Entertainia, and it's all for *our* little girl.

King (*nodding*) Yes, dear. But look at what it's costing us. The food, the champagne, the solid gold place settings for the fairy folk.

Queen Well you can't expect them to eat off common old porcelain, dear.

King (*gloomily*) No, I suppose not. But what about the new heated swimming pool? There was no need to buy one of those, was there?

Queen Oh, but look at the fun everyone had diving into it yesterday.

King They'd have had more if they'd waited till we'd had the water put in.

Queen No they *wouldn't*, silly. Most of them can't swim. (*She glances off* L) Oooooh, look at all that gorgeous food. Doesn't it make you feel hungry?

King Not really, dear. To tell you the truth, I seem to have lost my appetite.

Queen Oh, cheer up, Cedric. I'm sure one of the servants will find it for you. Now what's wrong? You haven't smiled once since you got up this morning.

King Oh, Semolina . . . I had an *awful* dream last night. Absolutely terrible. In fact it was so bad, I couldn't sleep a wink.

Queen (*concerned*) You poor darling. What was it about?

King I dreamed we were having a banquet, and there was nothing to eat but huge slabs of marshmallow.

Queen (*puzzled*) What's so terrible about that? You love marshmallow.

King I know, but when I opened my eyes, I'd eaten half the feather bed.

Queen Oh, my goodness. You don't feel sick, do you?

King No. Just down in the mouth.

Queen (*looking at him thoughtfully*) Cedric. You're not telling me everything, are you? There's something else. Come on. Out with it. Tell Semmi.

King Well ... if you *must* know ... I'm worried about money.

Queen (*surprised*) Money?

King Yes. We're spending far too much of it. If we're not careful, the entire country is going to be bankrupt. From now on, we've got to be very economical.

Queen But I'm always economical, dear. Look at the birthday cake I had made for my fortieth birthday. I only had twenty-three candles on it.

King I know, dear, but we've got to cut down further.

Queen Oh, I will. I will. Next year there'll be only twenty.

King (*groaning*) You don't understand, Semmi. Things are desperate. Only this morning the royal bank returned one of my cheques.

Queen (*delighted*) But that's *marvellous*, Cedric. That means we can use it to buy something else.

King No, no. It means we're overdrawn. We've taken too much money out. There's nothing left.

Queen (*firmly*) Then send it to another bank. They can't *all* be overdrawn.

King (*shaking his head*) We'll have to sell off some of our things. The royal yacht, the castle in Scotland, the suits of armour.

Queen (*dismayed*) Oh, no, Cedric. Not the armour. Besides, what would we charge for it?

King Eighteen pence an inch. It's first-class mail, you know. And the servants. We'll have to lose some of them, I'm afraid. There are far too many for us, anyway.

Queen (*wistfully*) I suppose that means I'll have to stop buying new dresses and things, too?

King (*nodding*) I'm afraid so. But if we manage to save a few pounds, perhaps we can afford to let you have a little *something*.

Queen (*brightening*) Oh, in that case, I'd better start thinking. Hmmmm. Supposing we got rid of all the chefs and I did the cooking myself? What would I get?

King My life insurance. Oh, Semmi, that's a terrible idea. You can't boil water without burning it, it takes you an hour to make instant coffee, and you're the only woman I know who tries to open an egg with a tin opener.

Queen Well, perhaps you're right. But I'm sure Dame Goodbody will help us out. What a marvellous cook *she* is. Only this morning she was telling me about a fabulous recipe she has for a senna pod casserole with fig and rhubarb sauce.

King Hmm. That should keep everybody going for a few days. Very well then. Have a word with her tonight and perhaps she can start tomorrow.

Fusspot enters

Fusspot (*bowing deeply*) If it pleases Your Majesties, the first of the guests are arriving.

Queen (*all of a flutter*) Oh, Cedric, I'm so nervous. Do I look all right?

King You look perfect, my dear. Now come along. We have to greet everyone as they arrive.

Queen Lead the way, Fussie. (*Suddenly letting out a shriek*) Ohhhhhhh.
King (*flustered*) What is it? What's wrong?
Queen (*in a panic*) My crown. My crown. I've lost my crown.
Fusspot But, it's on your head, Your Majesty.
Queen (*feeling for it*) Oh. (*Relieved*) Thank goodness you spotted it, Fussie. Another second and I'd have walked through there without it. (*To the King*) Well come along, Cedric. We have to do our duty.
King Yes, dear. (*To the Chamberlain*) You'd better tell Dame Goodbody to bring the baby down, Fusspot.
Fusspot Yes, Your Majesty. At once, Your Majesty. (*He bows deeply*)

The King and Queen exit down L

Now then. The nursery. (*Calling*) Dame Goodbody? Dame Goodbody?

He exits up R, *still calling. As he does so, Dame Goodbody enters down* R, *with the baby wrapped in a beautiful white lace shawl. She crosses to the cradle, chatting to the baby as she does so*

Dame (*brightly*) Here we are, my little princess. Into the cradle with you. (*She places the baby gently inside and tucks it up*) There. (*She beams*) Oooh, doesn't um look sweet? Now just you wait there till Nursey tells Mummy and Daddy you'se is all waiting for dem.

She turns away from the cradle just in time to see:

Tickles, who enters cheerfully down L

Oh, it's Tickles. (*She beams and waves coyly*) Oo-ooo.
Tickles (*giving a false smile*) Oh ... hello, Ammonia. I—er—I was just wondering where *you* were. Would—er—would you like me to get you a glass of champagne? (*He indicates off* L, *nervously*)
Dame (*simpering*) No, thank you. But I wouldn't mind a drop of that special sherry the queen likes so much.
Tickles Pale?
Dame No, just a glassful. (*She beams*) Then when you get back, perhaps we could have a little sit down and chat about our wedding plans.
Tickles (*startled*) *Wedding plans? What* wedding plans?
Dame (*smirking*) Oh, you don't fool *me*, Tickles. I know what you're up to. Chasing me all over the place, pretending to avoid me when somebody's watching—and keeping all the other young men away. You want to propose to me, don't you?
Tickles (*taken aback*) *I do?*
Dame (*smugly*) There. I knew it. You're desperately, passionately, over-whelmingly and madly in love with me, aren't you?
Tickles (*stunned*) *I am?*
Dame You see? I can read you like a book. You men are all alike, thank goodness. (*Airily*) Well, go on then. Down on your knees. Ask me to marry you.
Tickles But—but I don't *want* to marry you, Ammonia.
Dame Of course you do. I've just told you, haven't I? Now come on. Get on with it.

Tickles No. I don't think I should propose to you at all.
Dame (*surprised*) Why not?
Tickles Well . . . (*He thinks furiously*) . . . I've been hearing some very funny stories about you. That's why not.
Dame Funny stories?
Tickles Yes. I've been told that you're the biggest flirt in the kingdom. You've been on more knees than a linen serviette.
Dame Flatterer.
Tickles *And* you make a practice of kissing every man you can get your hands on.
Dame Well that's a lie. It's been years since I've needed practice.
Tickles But worst of all, they say you're a very jealous woman.
Dame (*taken aback*) Me? Jealous? Don't be ridiculous.
Tickles Well if you're not jealous why did you have men bridesmaids at your last wedding.
Dame (*simpering*) Oh, you don't want to go listening to all *those* silly stories. People are always spreading rumours about girls who are popular with the men.
Tickles I didn't know *you* were popular with men.
Dame Oh, yes. When I was at school, they voted me "The girl with whom you were most likely to succeed". (*She preens*) As a matter of fact, even now, there are two men fighting over me.
Tickles (*aside*) Yes. The loser gets her.
Dame Oh, come on. Be a devil. Propose to me.
Tickles I'm sorry, Ammonia, but it wouldn't be fair to you. You see, I might not be here for much longer. I'm fed up with being a jester so I'm going down to the police station to apply for another job.
Dame You can't be a policeman. You're not big enough.
Tickles Oh, I don't want to be a policeman. I'm applying for the other job. The one they're advertising on the board outside.
Dame What's that?
Tickles Man wanted for burglaries in Bradford.
Dame If anyone murdered you after a joke like that, the police'd have the entire audience as suspects. Now stop messing about, put your arms round me and lock on to this. (*She puckers up her lips for a kiss*)
Tickles (*quickly*) Too late. Look. All the guests are here. (*He points off* L)
Dame Oh, bother. Never mind. As soon as the party's over, we can carry on where we left off. These lips will still be waiting. (*She simpers and moves upstage, back towards the cradle*)

The guests begin to enter the ballroom. They fill out the background as Shout and Bawl, two very untidy looking Heralds, appear up L

Shout (*announcing loudly*) Their Royal Majesticals . . .
Bawl (*equally loudly*) King Cedric the Seventh and Queen Semolina.
Shout }
Bawl } (*together, imitating trumpets*) Taraaaaaaaaaaa.

All bow or curtsy as:

The King and Queen enter and take their places on the twin thrones

Shout and Bawl exit up L

Queen My husband and I——
King (*quickly*) Not now, Semmi. Not now.

Fusspot enters in great excitement, L

Fusspot (*bowing*) If it should please Your Majesties, the Fairy Folk have just arrived.

There is an excited reaction from all

King Show them in, Fussie. Show them in.

Fusspot quickly exits L

Queen Oh, Cedric. I can hardly believe it. Immortals here in *our* palace.
King I know. And I'm so nervous. They haven't visited earth in years. I do hope everything's to their liking.

Fusspot enters grandly

Fusspot The Fairy Azuriel and her companions.

Azuriel and the six Fairies enter R

The King and Queen rise to greet them. The Fairies form an attitude and all bow or curtsy deeply to them

King (*nervously*) Welcome to Entertainia, Your Fairynesses.
Azuriel   (*kindly*) We thank you, and with joyful hearts
                       Take leave of Fairy portals
                       To join your celebrations,
                       Most deserving of all mortals.
                       Upon the child in yonder crib
                       Our blessings we shall rain
                       That ev'ry day she'll sweeter grow.
                       Come, give her chosen name.
Queen Oh, well, to tell you the truth, Your Fairyship, we couldn't decide on one, so we thought we'd ask *you* to name her for us. If you wouldn't mind?
Azuriel   (*smiling*) Most gladly. Then from this day on,
                       Her name shall be, *Aurora.*

Everyone smiles with delight at the name

                       (To the other Fairies) Come sisters. Bless this tiny child
                       And lay your gifts before her.

Each Fairy approaches the cradle and waves her wand over it. With each blessing, all react with pleasure and excitement

1st Fairy   I give you Goodness. You'll never do wrong.
2nd Fairy   I give you Music, in speech and in song.
3rd Fairy   I give you Charm, and enhance it with grace.

4th Fairy   I give you Beauty, in figure and face.
5th Fairy   I give you Lightness in dancing a measure.
6th Fairy   I give you Love, which is life's greatest treasure.
Azuriel   And I, little princess, shall give you, my dear,
                   The gift of——

There is a bright flash and Carabosse appears down L. *She is an ancient, witch-like figure in rotting rags, supporting herself on a crooked stick. She is ugly, sharp eyed, and dangerously sweet*

All react

Carabosse   (*in mock surprise*) My goodness. What's going on here?
Fairies   (*dismayed*) Carabosse.
Carabosse   (*looking round*) It looks like a christening—but no. That can't be.
                  Or why was no invite extended to *me*? (*She looks thoughtful*)
Azuriel   (*stepping forward with a smile*) Dear sister, we greet you.
                  For many long year
                  We thought you were dead ...
                  Yet now you are here.
King   (*puzzled*) Who is she?
Carabosse   Oh, no-one *important*. Don't worry your head.
Azuriel   (*anxiously*) Dear sister, I beg you——
Carabosse   (*snapping viciously*) Be quiet, or you're *dead*. (*She glares at her*)

All react uneasily

                  (*Quietly but forcefully*) Now answer my question. I want a reply.
                  Why was ev'ryone asked to attend here but I?
                  Do you think, as I'm old, that to you I'm no loss?
                  Then you'll soon find it's risky to scorn Carabosse.
Azuriel   You *were* asked, dear sister, as so were we all.
                  Thrice welcome you are at this Christening Ball.
Carabosse   (*nodding*) Then all's well that ends well. I'm last but not least.
                  I'll willingly join in the christening feast.
Dame (*to Tickles*) Yes, she looks as though she could do with a good meal.
Queen (*to Fusspot*) Quickly. Set another place. Gold plate. Knife, fork and spoon.
Fusspot But that's impossible. Your Majesty. We only had seven made. All we have left is the pewter service.
Carabosse   (*eyes glittering*) Oh, dear. How upsetting. It's always the way
                  With guests *unexpected*, I'm sorry to say.
Azuriel   (*quickly*) Dear sister, take mine. I'll willingly wait.
Carabosse   (*airily*) No, no. Serve me *my* meal on any old plate.

> Some crusts of stale bread and a few scraps will do
> For an old hag like me.

Azuriel That's not true.

Fairies That's not true.

King Of course it isn't. You'll have exactly the same as everyone else.

Queen (*nodding*) Same food, same wine, sit at the same table.

Fusspot (*flustered*) Oh, dear, oh dear. This is *most* embarrassing. (*To the King and Queen*) Your Majesties ...

Both Yes?

Fusspot I—er—I'm afraid there's no room at the table. Every seat's taken.

All look dismayed except for Carabosse who smiles evilly

Carabosse (*sweetly*) No matter. No matter. No need to say more.
Just clear me a space and I'll dine on the floor.

King (*relieved*) Oh, *would* you? That'll solve ev——I mean, certainly *not*. We wouldn't hear of it, would we, Semmi? (*To Fusspot*) Chamberlain. Show this—er—er—lady to the kitchens. She can sit with the servants in front of the fire.

Azuriel (*dismayed*) Your Majesty——

Carabosse (*loudly*) Silence.

Everyone reels back with alarm

> (*To the King, coldly*) I thank you, my lord, for the
> *kindness* you offer.
> As payment, allow me *my* blessing to proffer.
> (*With great venom*) When your child is sixteen, I do now
> prophesy,
> On a spindle she'll prick herself, swoon and then *die*.

All react in horror

> I'll prove that it's folly to slight Carabosse.
> Fare you well, till the next time our paths have to cross.

There is a great flash and she vanishes off L

Everyone is left stunned and dismayed

Queen (*collapsing on to the throne*) Oh, Cedric. I'm going to have a conniption.

King (*subsiding on to his throne*) Make that two. I could do with a drink myself.

Dame (*to Azuriel*) Who *was* that? She looked like an accident searching for somewhere to happen.

Azuriel The eldest and most powerful of all in Fairyland,
But cruel, mean and spiteful and completely out of hand.
We thought her dead long years ago. It gave us quite a fright
To see her suddenly appear within this place tonight.

Tickles But—she didn't really *mean* what she said, did she? That the princess is going to die when she's sixteen?

Azuriel   Alas, I fear her wicked spell is well and truly cast.
                   The poor princess indeed will die when sixteen years have
                   passed.

Everyone looks dismayed

Dame (*clutching at her heart*) Oh, my poor little Aurora.
King (*to Azuriel*) Can't *you* do anything?
Azuriel   Our powers 'gainst those of Carabosse are infinitely small.
                   I much regret there's very little we can do at all.
                   (*Suddenly*)
                   But wait . . . Of *course*. I *can* give help to ease your pain
                   distressing.
                   Old Carabosse her spell did cast before the child received
                   my blessing.
                   Fear not, dear friends. All shall be well. No need for you
                   to weep.
                   Princess Aurora shall not die, but fall into enchanted
                   sleep,
                   And simply dream in perfect bliss till wakened by a
                   prince's kiss.

All react

King You mean she's not going to die after all?
Queen She'll just go to beddy-byes? (*Delightedly*) Oh, Cedric. (*She hugs him*)

All congratulate each other

Tickles (*suddenly*) Here, hang on a minute, though what would happen if there weren't any spindles lying around for the princess to prick her finger on?
Dame What are you talking about? We've got fifty of 'em here in the palace.
Tickles I know. But what if we *hadn't*? What if there were no spinning wheels left in the entire kingdom?
Dame Well it's obvious, isn't it? If there were no spinning wheels, she wouldn't be able to——— (*She realizes*) You're right. (*To the others*) He's right.
King (*jumping up excitedly*) He is. He is. The jester's right. If I give orders for all spinning wheels to be destroyed, we'd have nothing to worry about in any case.
Queen (*rising*) You must do it at *once*, Cedric. Immediately.
Fusspot The Queen is right, Your Majesty. The quicker the better.
King (*nodding*) Where are the heralds? They were here a few minutes ago.
Fusspot I'll summon them at once, sire.
King No, no. We've no time to waste. Just tell them to set out at once for the furthest corners of the kingdom and make this proclamation. (*Thinks*) By order of His Royal Majesty, King Cedric the Seventh, etc., etc., all spinning wheels must be destroyed before tomorrow morning. Anyone caught using one from this day on will be hung, drawn and quartered . . .

boiled in oil ... sliced into slivers ... burned at the stake ... and after that, we'll probably have them executed.

Everyone reacts

Fusspot I'll see to it at once, Your Majesty.

Fusspot bows and hurries off L

King (*relieved*) Oh, I feel happier already. (*To Tickles*) I'll see you're rewarded for this, Jester.
Queen Oh, Cedric. Thank goodness it's all ended happily. I'm so relieved, I think we should carry on with the celebrations.
Azuriel   (*smiling*) A good idea. So let's be merry, hale and hearty
                        And joy prevail at this christening party.

She waves her wand and everyone cheers loudly. There is a reprise of the opening song with everyone joining in. As it continues, Dame fondly lifts the baby out of the cradle and hands it to the Queen. The Queen accepts it with a beaming smile. Then her face changes to dismay as she realizes the baby has christened her. The scene ends in general merriment

SCENE 2

A corridor in the palace

Fusspot enters L, *looking flustered. He carries a rolled scroll*

Fusspot (*calling*) Heralds. Heralds. (*He looks around*) Oh, where are the wretched creatures? Never around when one wants one. (*Calling louder*) Heralds.

Shout and Bawl enter, one R *the other* L. *Shout carries a paper bag containing pastries*

Shout ⎱
Bawl ⎰ (*together*) Somebody calling?
Fusspot (*startled*) Who are you? (*He looks at them in distaste*)
Shout Shout——
Bawl —and Bawl.
Both At your service.
Shout Heralds to their Royal Magneticals, King Cedric the Seventh——
Bawl —and Queen Semolina.

They give clumsy bows

Fusspot (*spluttering*) But—but—I've never seen you before in my life.
Bawl (*cheerfully*) Course you haven't, old cock. We only started here tonight. We'll be in every Monday, Wednesday and Friday from now on.
Fusspot Why won't you be here, Sundays, Tuesdays, Thursdays and Saturdays?
Shout (*shrugging*) Nobody asked for daily heralds.

Fusspot (*dismayed*) Surely there must be some *smarter* heralds in the palace?

Bawl Not by this time, Mr Chamberpot. The smarter ones heard you shouting and hopped it.

Fusspot (*resignedly*) Oh very well. You'll have to do I suppose. Take this proclamation (*he hands it to Bawl*) and make sure everyone in the kingdom hears it.

Shout Leave it to us, Mr Fussperlain. We'll not let you down.

Fusspot I sincerely hope not. Now hurry along. And be back as quickly as you can.

Fusspot exits

Bawl (*to Shout*) Quick. Into the dining-room. See if we can get anything to eat before we set off. (*He tucks the scroll into his belt*)

Shout Don't you ever think of anything but food?

Bawl Course I do, but I don't half fancy one of them pastries. Mmmmmmmmm.

Shout Well, as it so happens, I managed to get a doughnut and a jam tart while no-one was looking, and I'll sell you one for ten pence.

Bawl Ten pence? Oh, all right, then. I'll have the doughnut.

Shout opens his paper bag and produces a doughnut which he hands over

(*Drooling*) Ooooh, I can't wait to get my teeth into this. I love doughnuts. (*Suddenly*) Hang about, though. Hang about. I've changed my mind. I'll have the jam tart instead.

He hands back the doughnut. Shout replaces it in the bag and gives him the jam tart in exchange

Shout Here you are. One jam tart.

Bawl Oooh, smashing. (*He opens his mouth to take a bite*)

Shout (*stopping him*) Hold on a minute. Hold on. What about the ten pence?

Bawl What ten pence?

Shout For the jam tart.

Bawl But I gave you the doughnut for it.

Shout Yes. I know you gave me the doughnut for it, but you didn't pay me for the doughnut, did you?

Bawl Course I didn't. I didn't eat it, did I? You don't expect me to pay for something I haven't had.

Shout (*snatching the tart back*) Give me that back. (*He puts it in the bag*)

Bawl Ooooh, you *mean* thing.

Shout No I'm not.

Bawl Yes you are. (*To the audience*) Isn't he, boys and girls?

Audience reaction

You see? (*Turning back to Shout*) You're *rotten*, you are. Absolutely rotten. (*To the audience*) Do you know, he's so mean, he makes his children take their glasses off when they're not looking at anything. Doesn't want them to wear out the lenses.

Shout (*pulling him back*) Shhhhh. You don't have to tell them things like that.

Bawl Yes, I do. I'm going to tell them about you, I am. *All* about you.

Shout (*affecting amusement*) Honestly, all this fuss because I wouldn't give you a little jam tart. All right then. I'll give you them *both*—on one condition.

Bawl What's that?

Shout That you have a little bet with me.

Bawl Little bet? What sort of little bet?

Shout I'll bet you one pound that you can't answer "pastries" every time I ask you a question.

Bawl (*scornfully*) I'll bet you I *can*.

Shout All right then. Put your pound down.

Bawl gets out a pound coin, and puts it at his feet

Bawl One pound.

Shout And here's the pastries. (*He puts the bag down by the coin*) Right. Are you ready?

Bawl I'm ready.

Shout crows with delight and picks up the coin

(*Startled*) Here, what are you doing?

Shout You didn't say "pastries", did you? (*He grins*)

Bawl Oh, that's not fair. I didn't realize we'd started. Let's do it again.

Shout All right. Put another pound down, then.

Bawl (*finding a coin and putting it down*) One pound.

Shout Are you ready to start now?

Bawl Pastries. (*He beams*)

Shout There. That was easy, wasn't it?

Bawl Like falling off a log.

Shout picks up the coin with a laugh

(*Realizing*) Oooooh. Do it again. Do it again.

Shout For the last time then.

Bawl puts down a coin

Are you ready?

Bawl Pastries.

Shout You got it right *that* time, didn't you?

Bawl Pastries.

Shout Which would you rather have—the pound coin or the pastries?

Bawl Pastries.

Shout In that case you can have them—and I'll have the money.

Shout snatches up the coin and runs off

Bawl picks up the bag with a smirk, then realizes

With a howl of rage he chases off after Shout

SCENE 3

The palace gardens. A scorching hot day, sixteen years later

It is a very beautiful garden, crowded with trees, shrubs and glorious blossoms. The palace can be seen in the background. There is a large garden seat L

The Lights come up on Princess Aurora singing happily with the Courtiers and palace children dancing with her

Song 3 (Aurora and Courtiers)

At the end of the song all slump with exhaustion, laughing and fanning themselves. The Princess sits on the garden seat

Girl (*breathlessly*) Oh, Your Highness, isn't it *hot* today?
Princess (*fanning herself with her hand*) I know. What I wouldn't give for a nice cool glass of Dame Goodbody's lemonade.

All agree heartily

Boy I'll go to the kitchen and ask her if she'll make some.
Girl No. I'll go.
2nd Girl I'll go.
2nd Boy No. I'll go.
Princess (*laughing*) You can *all* go.

  Everyone hurries off with much excitement

  (*Calling*) And don't forget it was my idea.

She lays back on the seat, softly singing a few bars of the song. A moment later, the Queen's voice is heard off R

Queen (*off, calling*) Aurora?

  The Queen enters, followed by the King

  (*Beaming*) Oh, there you are, dear. We were wondering where you'd got to. (*She crosses to her*)
King We've been searching everywhere.
Princess (*sitting up*) I'm sorry. But it was so hot inside the palace. I just had to come outside for a breath of fresh air.
Queen (*sitting beside her*) Well, I must say it makes a change from yesterday. It was so foggy all day, we never got a chance to see what the weather was like. If you ask me, the weather this year's been more unusually unusual than the usual unusual weather we usually get.
King (*blinking*) Er ... yes, dear. (*Briskly*) Well, never mind. It's absolutely perfect weather for our little girl's birthday, and that's all that matters. (*He beams at Aurora*)
Princess (*smiling*) Not a little girl any more, Father. I'm sixteen years old today. Almost fully grown.
Queen (*sighing*) Sweet sixteen. Oh, I can hardly believe it. It seems like only yesterday I held you in my arms for the very first time.

Princess Was I a happy baby, Mother?

Queen Oh, yes, my dear. And pretty as a picture.

King Everyone said you looked exactly like *me*. (*He attempts to look modest*)

Queen (*nodding*) But you were healthy enough, so we didn't worry.

The King reacts

Oh, I'll never forget how we used to climb the stairs to the nursery each night to feed you those lovely big boiled onions.

Princess (*surprised*) Boiled onions? Whatever for?

King Well, the nursery was so large, it was the only way we could find you in the dark.

Princess (*laughing*) Oh, Father. You are funny. You make me laugh almost as much as Tickles.

King Tickles? Tickles? Don't talk to me about Tickles. I'm very annoyed with *him*. Do you know, he threw away this morning's paper before I'd even had a chance to read it.

Queen (*rising*) Oh, dear. You musn't blame poor Tickles for *that*, Cedric. (*She looks guilty*) That was *my* fault. I used it to wrap all the scraps from the breakfast table, and told him to put it in the dustbin.

King (*protesting*) Semmi, how could you? You knew I'd want to see it.

Queen But there wasn't much to see, dear. Just egg-shells, grapefruit skins, bacon rinds and some bits of dry toast.

King No, no, no. I meant I wanted to see the *paper*. How can I be expected to run the country if I don't know what's going on around me? I might as well be a Member of Parliament. (*He moves down* R)

Queen (*following*) Oh, *I* can give you all the news, dear. I made notes of all the important things that have happened since yesterday. For instance, there was a big robbery at the local wig factory last night and the thieves stole two tons of human hair.

King (*turning to her*) Why on earth would anyone want to steal two tons of human hair?

Queen I've no idea, Cedric, but detectives are combing the area.

The King reacts

Oh, and there was another burglary in *Scotland*.

King (*interested*) Scotland?

Queen (*nodding*) Some wicked person broke into a public house and stole the charity pile of pennies.

King (*indignantly*) Disgraceful. Absolutely scandalous.

Queen Yes. That's just what I thought too. But not to worry. The police will soon catch him. Both pennies were marked, you see.

The Princess giggles

King (*clearing his throat*) Ahem. That—er— that's all very well, Semmi, but what I really wanted was the political news.

Queen Well, there wasn't very much of that, thank goodness. (*She thinks*) Now let me see ... Oh, yes. The Government have just announced that they've finally found a way to shorten the dole queues.

King And about time too. Did they say what it was?

Queen They're going to ask everyone to stand closer together.

King (*at a loss*) Hmmm. Yes. Well, I—er—I don't think *that* information is going to be much use to me. Perhaps I'd better go listen to the news on that new radio we were presented with last week.

Queen (*amused*) Don't be silly, Cedric. It's a Japanese radio. You won't be able to understand a word. Besides, I won't have you thinking about work today. It's Aurora's birthday and we're going to do nothing but enjoy ourselves. You run along and inspect the guards whilst I take Aurora inside to try on the gown she's going to wear for the party tonight.

Princess (*jumping up*) Oh, *must* I, Mother? (*She hurries down to her*) There's simply hours before the party begins and it's so stuffy inside.   Couldn't I stay out here for just a while longer?

Queen (*fondly*) Oh, very well, then. But don't sit directly in the sun. We don't want you getting sunstroke, do we? (*To the King*) Come along, Cedric. (*Coyly*) You can chase me round the corridors.

King I'd never be able to catch you.

Queen Don't worry. I'll dawdle.

The Queen giggles and exits quickly up R. *The King beams and hurries after her*

Princess (*laughing*) Dear old mother and father. Still as romantic as ever. (*She yawns*) Oh, dear, I do feel tired. It must be all this sunshine. (*She moves back to the seat and sits*) I'm so thirsty, too. They're taking an awful long time with that lemonade. (*She yawns*) Oh, it's so pleasant sitting here with nothing but the sounds of nature to disturb me. (*Her head begins to droop*) Birds singing . . . bees humming . . . the scent of the flowers . . . (*She falls asleep*)

Soft music begins

Two huge butterflies enter and flutter around the garden. They are quickly followed by other insects and eventually a graceful ballet of insects begins

Music (Insect Ballet)

At the end of the ballet the insects exit silently

There is a flash

Carabosse appears L, *bathed in a green light. She sees Aurora*

Carabosse　　　(*moving close to her*) Now dawns the day of sweet revenge.
　　　　　　　　　The sixteen years have passed.
　　　　　　　　　Since I decreed this fair princess
　　　　　　　　　Would come to grief, and breath her last.
　　　　　　　　　In vain they seek to thwart my plan.
　　　　　　　　　This child whom they so cherish,
　　　　　　　　　Tonight, I vow, will meet her fate
　　　　　　　　　And by a spindle perish. (*She cackles with glee*)

Azuriel enters R

Azuriel   Not so, dear sister Carabosse. Your evil plan will fail.
                   Princess Aurora shall not die. *My* magic will prevail.
                   Within a rose filled bower, the time she'll merely dream
                     away,
                   Till wakened by a prince's kiss; yet growing lovelier ev'ry
                     day.
Carabosse   (*furious*) A curse on you, Azuriel. How dare you
                     interfere?
                   An enemy you've made of me. That slip will cost you
                     dear.
                   You think to spoil my fun but you'll discover by and by
                   That Carabosse will have her way, whatever tricks you
                     try. (*She sneers*)
                   No prince shall kiss her ruby lips, I'm sorry to relate,
                   And though she sleeps ten thousand years—I swear death
                     still shall be her fate.

Carabosse swirls around and exits L

Azuriel   (*to the audience*) Alas, I fear old Carabosse is still on
                     mischief bent.
                   There seems to be no hope at all, she'll soften and relent;
                   But though her spiteful actions may bring temporary
                     sorrow,
                   I guarantee all shall be well, in some long distant morrow.
                   As for today, a special gift I bring this princess fair.
                   (*To Aurora*)
                   Just wish for what your heart desires. In moments 'twill
                     be there.

Azuriel waves her wand and exits R

The Lights return to normal

Fusspot (*off* R, *calling*) Your Highness? Your Highness? Where are you?

Aurora awakes with a start. She rubs her eyes

Fusspot enters R, *holding a goblet on a small tray*

Oh, *there* you are. (*He crosses to her*) I've brought your lemonade.
Princess (*smiling as she rises*) Thank you, Fussie. (*She yawns*) I must have
fallen asleep. (*She takes the goblet and drinks*) Mmmm.
Fusspot (*with a pained expression*) Your Highness is fortunate. *I* haven't had
a good sleep in ages. I think I must have insomnia.
Princess (*concerned*) Poor Fussie. How awful. (*She moves down* C) Have
you tried counting sheep? I hear that's supposed to help.
Fusspot (*following her down*) Perhaps so, Your Highness, but it didn't work
for me. (*He sighs*) First of all I counted *white* sheep, but it made me so
tired I had to give up, so then I tried counting *black* sheep and that was
absolutely hopeless.

Princess Why was that?

Fusspot Well, it was so dark, I couldn't even see them. (*Wearily*) I've even tried laying on the edge of my bed to see if I could drop off, but nothing happened. Whatever can be wrong with me?

Princess Perhaps there's something worrying you, Fussie? That *could* be the answer, you know.

Fusspot (*interested*) Really? Well, now you come to mention it, there *is* something that's giving me cause for concern. You see, for the past few weeks I haven't been able to wear my blue and white striped pyjamas when I go to bed. I have to wear my bathing costume.

Princess Whatever for?

Fusspot There's a leak in my hot water bottle.

The Princess laughs

(*Shrugging*) Still, I suppose that once their majesties are able to pay my wages again, I'll be able to afford a new one.

Princess (*suddenly contrite*) Poor Fussie. It seems terrible not to be able to pay you when we're throwing this big birthday party tonight.

Fusspot Not at all. Not at all. There's no need to get upset. None of us mind having to do without. We all love you very much, you see, and besides, you've got to have a party. Their majesties have invited every prince for miles around. (*He smiles*) Who knows? One of them may fall in love with you and ask for your hand in marriage. (*He sighs dreamily*)

Princess Do you think so, Fussie? Really and truly?

Fusspot But of course. You're the most beautiful girl in the world and growing lovelier every day. How could he help it?

Princess And how would I know I'd fallen in love with *him*? (*She drinks*)

Fusspot Oh you'd know, Your Highness. You'd know. (*He snaps out of it*) But I'd better be getting back inside. There's all sorts of things to do before the guests start arriving, and if I'm not there to organize ...

Aurora replaces the goblet on the tray

Fusspot hurries off up R

Princess (*sighing*) If only I *could* meet a handsome prince with lots of money. I'm sure it would solve all our problems. The trouble is, every wealthy prince I've met so far has been fat and unpleasant. I'm quite sure I could never fall in love with any of *them*. If I could be sure the right man would come along eventually, I wouldn't mind waiting till I'm quite old — maybe thirty, or so. Oh, I *wish* I could meet the man I *am* going to marry, if only for a few minutes.

There is a flickering of the Lights and Aurora throws up her hands to shield her eyes. There is a flash

Prince Valiant appears down R. *He is young and handsome, and dressed in a style of costume worn in the seventeenth century*

(*Startled*) Who are *you*?

Prince (*equally startled*) What? (*He looks around quickly*) Oh. (*Dazedly*) I

... er ... Prince Valiant of Euphoria ... richest country in the whole world. (*He gives her an uncertain bow*) But where am I?

Princess (*staring at him*) Inside the palace gardens.

Prince But that's impossible. I know every inch of the gardens, and I've certainly never seen *this* place before.

Princess Perhaps not, but that's where you are. Look. (*She indicates*) There's the palace behind you.

Prince (*looking at it in bewilderment*) But—but that's not *my* palace.

Princess (*amused*) Well of course it isn't. It's the royal palace of Entertainia.

Prince Entertainia? (*He turns to look at her again*) You're making fun of me.

Princess Why should I?

Prince Entertainia's just a legend. It doesn't exist.

Princess (*laughing*) Whatever gave you that idea? Of course it exists. It's one of the oldest kingdoms on earth.

Prince (*putting his fingers to his temples*) What am I doing here?

Princess (*frowning*) Can't you remember?

Prince (*helplessly*) No.

Princess (*thoughtfully*) Well, you are a bit *early*, but perhaps you were coming to my birthday party?

Prince (*shaking his head*) I don't think so. In fact, the last thing I do remember, I was sitting in the garden reading one of those dusty old books from Father's library, and thinking how tired I was. (*His face lights up*) Of course. That's it, isn't it? I'm dreaming all this. I must have fallen asleep.

Princess You don't seem very asleep to *me*.

Prince Well, I wouldn't, would I? Because *you're* part of my dream. You wouldn't notice *anything* unusual about me. That's what's so strange about dreams. Everything seems so real in them. These gardens ... that palace ... you.

Princess (*laughing*) But we *are* real.

Prince (*shaking his head*) No, no. You're not. I only wish you were. You see no real person could be as beautiful as you are. You have to be a dream. (*He moves down* L, *thinking*) Now let me think. If this is Entertainia, and that's the royal palace over there, you must be Princess Aurora. Am I right?

Princess Yes.

Prince (*turning to her*) And your father and mother must be ... King Cedric the Seventh and Queen Semolina. (*He moves back towards her*)

Princess That's right. Do you know them?

Prince (*laughing*) Let's say I know *of* them. That's probably why I'm dreaming I'm standing here talking to you.

Princess I don't understand.

Prince It's simple. You were all in the book I was reading just before I fell asleep ... *Mysterious Stories of the Golden Age*.

Princess (*puzzled*) I don't think I've ever heard of that.

Prince (*quickly*) Oh, no. You wouldn't have done. It wasn't written till long after you'd supposedly fallen under the wicked fairy's spell and the Kingdom of Entertainia vanished.

Princess Vanished?

Prince (*lightly*) Silly, isn't it? Here I am talking to you as though you were really by my side. I can hear the rustle of your gown and smell the beautiful perfume you're wearing. It's the most amazing dream I've ever had, and I hope I'm not going to forget it when I wake up. (*Gently*) You're even more beautiful than the book describes you.

Princess (*a little afraid*) I think I'd better be going inside. Excuse me. (*She turns to exit up* R)

Prince (*urgently*) No. Please don't go.

She hesitates

I want to remember this dream for the rest of my life, but most of all, I want to remember you.

Princess Well I'll certainly remember *you*. You're the strangest person I've ever met. If I didn't know better I'd think *I* was dreaming too.

Prince Maybe you are. Maybe the whole world is just one long dream, but if that's so, I'd like to get to know you better before I wake up again. After all, it may be the last time I'll ever see you.

Princess I hope not. I really hope not.

Prince So do I.

Song 4 (Prince and Princess)

At the end of the song, Tickles is heard calling, off R

Tickles (*off*) Princess? Oh, Princess.

The Princess turns to greet Tickles

Prince Valiant is whisked off L, *without the Princess noticing. Tickles enters* R

(*To the audience*) Hiya, kids. (*To the Princess*) Hello, Princess. I was hoping to find you on your own.

Princess (*puzzled*) On my own? (*She looks round and sees the Prince has gone*) Oh.

Tickles (*curious*) Something wrong?

Princess He's gone. (*She looks anxiously about*)

Tickles Who has?

Princess The young man I was talking to a moment ago. Prince Valiant.

Tickles Prince Valiant? (*Blankly*) I didn't see any Prince Valiant.

Princess (*protesting*) But you must have done. He was right there. (*She indicates*) He was wearing (*she describes the costume the Prince wore*).

Tickles (*eyeing her strangely*) Are you sure you didn't imagine him, Princess. You wouldn't catch anybody round here walking about looking like that. Not unless he was going to a fancy dress party.

Princess (*impatiently*) Of course I didn't imagine him. I saw him. Spoke to him. (*Dreamily*) Oh, Tickles, he was the handsomest man I've ever seen.

Tickles Oh. Well—perhaps he's gone for a walk round the gardens?

Princess (*eagerly*) Do you think so? Oh, quickly, Tickles. Go after him. I've just got to see him again.

Tickles Don't worry, Princess. You'll see him at the party tonight, won't you? I mean, if he's a prince, he's bound to be there. All the rest of them will be.

Princess (*relieved*) Oh, yes. Of course. The party. I'd almost forgotten about that.

Tickles (*surprised*) Your own birthday party? How could you forget a thing like that? Here, and that reminds me. That's why I was looking for you. (*Shyly*) I've brought you a present.

Princess (*touched*) Oh, Tickles. You haven't.

Tickles I have.

Princess You *haven't*.

Tickles (*frowning*) Haven't I? (*He thinks*) Yes, I have. (*Awkwardly*) It isn't very much, but I've been saving up my pocket money for it since the day you were born. (*He gets a small ring box out of his tunic*) Here.

Princess (*opening it eagerly*) Oh, Tickles. It's beautiful. A diamond ring. Is it real?

Tickles If it isn't, I've been diddled out of fifty p. Yes, it's a real one, Princess. And just in case you're wondering why it's such a *small* diamond, well, it's because I didn't want the glare to hurt your eyes.

Princess (*doubtfully*) The only thing is, I'm not sure I ought to accept it. After all, I wouldn't want Dame Goodbody to be upset.

Tickles Why should she be?

Princess She is your fiancée, and I don't believe you bought her anything for *her* last birthday.

Tickles Yes, I did. I did. I asked her what she wanted and she told me something for her neck, so I bought her a bar of soap.

Princess And what did you buy her for Chistmas?

Tickles Er ... A Zulu washing machine.

Princess (*laughing*) You mean a Zanussi washing machine.

Tickles No. A Zulu. It was a big flat rock. (*He mimes pounding washing*)

Dame Goodbody enters R

Dame Oh, there you are, Aurora. Run along into the palace, dear. Mother's waiting for you to try on the new frock I've made.

Tickles (*quickly*) I—I'll come with you, Princess. Help you with the hooks and eyes.

Dame Never mind the hooks and eyes. I want a word with you. (*To the Princess*) Off you go, dear.

The Princess smiles then exits up R

Tickles (*groaning*) Oh, don't start again, Ammonia. I know exactly what you're going to say. (*Mocking her*) When are we going to get married?

Dame Exactly. When *are* we going to get married? We blighted our trough sixteen years ago, and it's about time we had our nuptials attended to. I don't intend waiting for ever, you know. I want to be married again before I'm twenty.

Tickles But I've already told you. I can't afford to get married. I'm so poor, I can't even afford a new pair of shoes. I've had to paint my feet black and lace up my toes.

Dame Haven't you put anything away for a rainy day?

Tickles Course I have. I'm not stupid. I've got an umbrella and a pair of wellingtons.

Dame (*rolling her eyes*) And to think I could have married any man I pleased.

Tickles (*to the audience*) The trouble was, she never found anybody she *did* please.

Dame Oh, no? Well for your inflammation, you're not the only man who's got his eye on me. (*Smugly*) The Lord Chamberlain's been popping in to sample my accomplishments every time you've had your back turned.

Tickles (*surprised*) Oooh, the snake in wolf's clothing. (*Indignantly*) Now just you listen to me, Ammonia Goodbody. You don't want to have anything to do with old Fusspot.

Dame Why not? There's many a good tune played on an old fiddle. Besides, he's charming, polite, good looking—and he's got very good manners. He always takes his shoes off before he puts his feet on the table.

Tickles He—er—he hasn't kissed you yet, has he?

Dame Well . . . no. But he *has* steamed up my glasses a couple of times.

Tickles (*annoyed*) I knew it. I knew it. I can't let you out of my sight without you go chasing after another man.

Dame (*triumphantly*) Ahaaaa. And who's jealous now, eh? (*Easily*) Anyway, you don't have to worry. I was making it all up. You're not the only one who can invent things.

Tickles (*disgustedly*) Oh, don't talk to me about inventions. I haven't been able to invent anything since old Fusspot made me promise not to. Sixteen years ago. And just when I was about to make a fortune.

Dame (*startled*) Eh? Make a fortune? How? What did you invent?

Tickles Oh, it was just a thing that let people look through solid brick walls as though they weren't there.

Dame (*impressed*) Good heavens. And what did you call it?

Tickles A window.

Dame (*to the audience*) I should have seen through that one. (*To Tickles*) Listen, potato-brain. If you haven't invented anything for sixteen years, what's that great big machine you've got hidden away at the top of the East Tower?

Tickles (*startled*) Shhhhhh. (*He looks around quickly*) Nobody's supposed to know about that.

Dame Why? What is it?

Tickles (*lowering his voice*) A time machine.

Dame (*in a normal voice*) A time machine? You mean a big alarm clock?

Tickles No, no, Ammonia. It's a machine that allows people to travel through time, back into the mysterious past.

Dame (*scornfully*) Don't be daft. There's no such thing. (*Interested*) Does it work?

Tickles Of course it works. Only last night I went back to *your* childhood to see what you looked like when you were a little girl. (*He smiles*) Oh, you were ever so pretty. You had a pink dress on, with yellow bows all down the front, and your hair done up in little plaits.

Dame Oooh. I remember that. (*She simpers*) I must have been about ten years old at the time. And did you speak to me?

Tickles Well, I was going to, but I had to make a quick getaway. The Roman invasion started.

Dame (*hurt*) There you go again. Making fun of me. Oh, I wish I were dead. (*She begins to sob*)

Tickles (*contrite*) Oh, don't cry, Ammonia. I didn't mean it. You know I really love you.

Dame No I don't.

Tickles Yes you do. I love you terribly.

Dame You can say that again. (*She sniffles*) Well if you do love me, how about giving me a great big romantic, juicy kiss?

Tickles What, on the sly? (*He looks to see no-one is watching*)

Dame No. On the lips. Here, and before you do, you've got to promise you won't ever tell a soul you did it.

Tickles Don't worry. I'll be just as ashamed of it as you.

Song 5 (Tickles and Dame)

At the end of the song there is a Black-out

Both exit

SCENE 4

A corridor in the palace

Shout and Bawl enter and stand extreme R

Shout ⎫ (*announcing together*) Their Royal Municipals, King Cedric the
Bawl ⎭ Seventh and Queen Semolina. Taraaaaaaaaaa.

The King and Queen enter R

Queen Oh, I hope everything's going to be all right, Cedric. If anything happens to Aurora, I don't know what we'll do.

King There, there, there. What could possibly happen? You know the precautions we've taken. Now stop worrying.

Queen (*sighing*) I can't help it. I've got this terrible feeling that that nasty old Carabosse is going to pop up again tonight.

King (*firmly*) Huh. Just let her try it and she'll see what happens. I've given strict instructions that no-one is to be admitted to the palace unless they've got a written invitation, and just in case she *does* decide to pay us a visit, I've invited that nice Fairy Azuriel to come along too.

Queen Do you think we ought to warn Aurora, though? Just to be on the safe side?

King Certainly not. We don't want to frighten her, do we? After all, she knows nothing about Carabosse and the wicked spell she cast, and besides, how can she prick her finger on the spindle of a spinning wheel? There isn't one in the country. Not even a picture of one.

Queen (*brightening*) Yes, you're right, dear. And in any case, we've got dozens of princes standing by, haven't we? The minute she closed her eyes, they'd be fighting for the chance to kiss her and wake her up again.

King Of course they would dear. Of course they would.

Queen (*thoughtfully*) You know, I've often wondered about the first time *you* kissed *me*.

King (*anxiously*) Shhhh. Not in front of the servants.

Queen (*lowering her voice*) I mean, who *told* you you could kiss me?

King Well—er—just about everybody. (*Quickly*) I mean ... How could I have resisted. You were the prettiest girl I'd ever seen.

Queen But I was only a poor telephone operator.

King I know. But when you walked across the ballroom towards me, I could see all your lines were engaged. And what a dancer. I'd never seen anyone Charleston so fast in my life.

Queen *Charleston?* (*Realizing*) Oh, I wasn't doing the Charleston, dear. The waiter had just spilled hot soup down my back.

The Princess enters

Princess (*hurrying to them*) Oh, Mother, Father. I've just met the most wonderful young man.

King Pardon?

Princess He was in the garden. Wandering around.

Queen (*puzzled*) Did he say what his name was?

Princess (*dreamily*) Oh, yes. Prince Valiant of Euphoria.

Queen (*frowning*) I don't remember inviting *him* to the party.

King (*puzzled*) Euphoria? *Euphoria?* I've never heard of it.

Princess It's the richest country in the whole world, Father.

Queen (*impressed*) Oooooh. (*Suddenly*) Country? (*She frowns*) I always thought Euphoria was a *state*.

King Anyway, what was he doing wandering around the garden?

Princess He didn't seem to know. (*Quickly*) But he's the handsomest young man I've ever seen and he says the *funniest* things. I can't *wait* to see him again.

King Er—what do you mean, the—er—the funniest things? What kind of things?

Princess (*amused*) Well, he pretended he was dreaming and said I was even more beautiful than the book described me.

Queen *Which* book?

Princess The one he said he was reading before he fell asleep. (*She laughs*) He told me I was going to fall under a wicked fairy's spell and Entertainia would vanish.

King }
Queen } (*together*) Aaaaagh. (*They clutch at each other*)

Princess (*startled*) What's the matter? What's wrong?

King (*recovering*) Oh ... it ... er ... it's nothing, dear. Just a touch of lumbago.

Queen (*whispering to the King*) It's *her*, Cedric. That Carabosse creature. She's out in the garden disguised as a prince. What are we going to do?

King (*in a panic*) Don't panic. Don't panic. (*Whispering*) We'll have her arrested and thrown into the dungeons till Azuriel arrives. Come on. (*Aloud to Aurora*) Have to dash, dear. We've just remembered something important. (*He begins to pull the Queen off* L)

Queen Stay inside the palace, darling. You'll be perfectly safe here.

The King and Queen both exit quickly

Princess (*staring after them puzzled*) Safe? Whatever did she mean?

Shout (*relaxing and coming forward*) Dunno. But they both looked a bit worried, didn't they?

Bawl (*moving forward*) Turned white as sheets.

Princess Perhaps I'd better go after them?

Shout No. They'll be all right. (*Eagerly*) Here, tell us about this prince you met in the garden.

Bawl A bit of all right, is he?

Princess Oh, *yes*. (*She sighs deeply*) I never imagined a man could be so attractive.

Shout (*airily*) Oh, I don't know. I'm not *too* bad looking meself.

Bawl No, you're not. Except for the blemish between your ears.

Shout What blemish?

Bawl Your face.

Shout Huh. You've some need to talk. Your eyes are so crossed, you can watch a tennis match without moving your head.

Princess (*firmly*) Now stop it, you two. That's enough. If you don't behave I won't tell you about Prince Valiant.

Shout
Bawl } (*together*) Sorry, Princess.

Princess Now what do you want to know?

Shout Well, is he the sort of feller you've always wanted to meet?

Bawl And do you think you've fallen in love with him?

Princess (*thoughtfully*) Fallen in love? I'm not quite sure, but I rather think I may have done.

Song 6 (Princess)

At the end of the song there is a Black-out

  All exit

SCENE 5

The great ballroom. Evening

The set is the same as Scene 1 but without the cradle

The Lights come up on the ballroom aglitter and Guests in rich costumes chatting excitedly or singing as a group of Dancers swirl around to the strains of a majestic waltz

Song 7 (Guests and Dancers)

Tickles enters up R *as the music ends*

Tickles Hiya kids.

Audience reaction

Cor, what a smashing party. Look at all the fancy clothes. They must have had a sale at Oxfam. And what posh people. There's one woman over there who's so stuck-up she won't have a local anaesthetic—she has all her's imported. (*He looks off*) And look at this one coming in now. I've never seen such a stupid looking ... blimey. It's Ammonia.

The Dame enters in a fantastic glittering costume

Dame (*calling gaily*) Yoo-hoo. Tickles. (*She glides towards him*)

Tickles (*looking her up and down*) Where on earth did you get that from?

Dame (*she names a local dress shop*) It was one of their discounts.

Tickles Looks more like one of their discards.

Dame Oh, I've never seen the shop so crowded. In fact it was so bad, five of us were trying on the same pair of corsets. Anyway, do you like it? (*She turns around to let him get a better look*)

Tickles Like it? It's absolutely terrible. It doesn't suit you at all.

Dame Of course it does. The saleswoman told me it matched my eyes. Perfectly. (*She flutters her lashes at him*)

Tickles She was pulling your leg. That colour's not a bit like bloodshot.

Dame Anyway, I got it for a ridiculous figure.

Tickles You can say that again. (*He sniffs suddenly and makes a face*) Ooooh.

Dame What's wrong?

Tickles (*examining the soles of his shoes*) That smell. What is it?

Dame (*simpering*) Oh, you've noticed. It's my new perfume. It's called "High Heaven".

Tickles Yes, and it certainly smells to it.

Dame (*seductively*) It's made from a secret recipe known only to the Nasturtium monks, and it's been handed down from father to son for hundreds and hundreds of years.

Tickles (*scornfully*) Give over.

Dame It's true. Nobody but them knows what's in it, but they do say that *one* of the ingredients is the pollen of an exotic flower that blooms only once every thousand years, and has to be collected when the moon is in Scorpio and the (*local bus service*) runs on time. They sell it in Boots Chemist at fivepence a bucketful.

Shout and Bawl enter up R

Shout ⎫ (*together*) Their Royal Adjectives, the King and Queen. Tar-
Bawl ⎭   aaaaaaa.

The King and Queen enter up R

All defer to them

Queen (*wincing*) I *do* wish we could afford real trumpets, Cedric.

The King and Queen move down C. *Shout and Bawl position themselves either side of the twin thrones*

King (*to everyone*) Carry on. Carry on. Enjoy yourselves.

Everyone resumes their conversation

(*Glancing around*) Now what's happened to old Fusspot?
Queen (*glancing off* L) Here he comes now.

Fusspot enters looking flustered

King Well?
Fusspot We've searched every inch of the grounds, Your Majesty, but there wasn't a sign of a prince anywhere. Are you sure the princess wasn't mistaken?
King Of course I'm sure. If Aurora says there was a prince in the garden, then a prince in the garden there was.
Tickles Here, you're not looking for that Prince Valiant, are you? The one she was talking to this afternoon?
Queen Why, yes. Did you see him too?
Tickles No. But she told me they were talking and suddenly he disappeared.
Fusspot Disappeared? (*Frowning*) Disappeared? (*Suddenly remembering*) Wait. Wait. I have it, sire. I have it.
King (*edging away*) Is it catching?
Fusspot (*eagerly*) No, no, sire. I mean I have the answer. When *I* saw the princess this afternoon, she'd just woken up from a little sleep. Perhaps she *dreamed* she saw this prince?
Queen (*relieved*) Of course. Oh, Cedric. Fussie's right. There wasn't a prince at all.
King But—she seemed so certain. And the things he told her.
Dame Oh, you don't want to worry about that. Dreams can be so real at times, they can frighten you. Why, only last week *I* dreamed I'd died and gone to my eternal rest.
Tickles Yes, but the heat down there soon woke her up again. (*He chuckles*)

The Dame snatches off his cap and hits him with it

King (*reluctantly*) Well, I suppose it *is* possible. And no-one's been able to find him. (*Deciding*) Yes. That *must* be the answer. The poor child was dreaming. Oh, what a relief. For one awful moment I thought she——
Shout ⎫ (*together*) Her Royal Highness, the Princess Aurora. Taraaaaaaaa.
Bawl ⎭

The Princess enters up R *in a beautiful gown*

As she moves C, *all smile and applaud her and sing "Happy Birthday". The Princess looks overwhelmed and moves from group to group to give her thanks. The Queen suddenly bursts into tears*

King (*anxiously*) What is it, Semmi? What's the matter?

Queen (*sniffling*) Oh, it's nothing, Cedric. It's just that every time I see someone looking so beautiful, I just have to cry. (*She mops her eyes*)

King (*sniffling*) I know. I feel the same way myself.

Fusspot I too can hardly control myself. If I wasn't the Lord Chamberlain, I'm sure I'd give a very loud wolf whistle. (*He looks embarrassed*)

Tickles Well when *I* see a really beautiful girl, I want to rush over to her and give her a great big kiss. What do you do, Ammonia?

Dame Oh, I just look at her for a few minutes, then get tired and put the mirror down.

The Princess comes down to join them

Princess (*anxiously*) I can't seem to see him anywhere.

Queen See who, dear?

Princess Prince Valiant. (*She looks round the ballroom again*)

The others exchange quick glances

King Ah, yes. I mean . . . no. That is . . . well . . . perhaps he hasn't arrived yet?

Princess (*disappointed*) Oh.

Fusspot (*beaming*) But there's plenty of time, Your Highness. The party's hardly begun.

Queen Fussie's right, dear. There's simply *hours* to go yet.

Tickles What about playing some party games? (*Aside to the King*) It might take her mind off him for a while.

King (*softly to him*) Good idea. (*Aloud*) What shall we play?

Dame How about Jockey's Knock?

Tickles (*frowning*) How do you play that?

Dame The same way as Postman's Knock, only there's a bit more horse-play.

Fusspot Why not Hide and Seek? I'm sure we all know *that*.

All agree

King (*turning to the Guests; brightly*) Hide and Seek, everyone. Hide and Seek.

All react delightedly

Queen (*gaily*) And as it's Aurora's party, *she* can be the one to hide.

All agree

Princess But——

Tickles (*firmly*) No buts, Princess. Off you go.

Dame We're only going to count up to ten.

Princess (*flustered*) Oh.

All (*counting*) One. Two. Three.

The Princess whirls around and exits up R *in a flurry of petticoats*

Four. Five. Six. Seven. Eight. Nine. *Ten.*

With much excitement, all exit. As the stage empties, Aurora hurries on again down R and exits up L. Several Guests follow her a moment later. Aurora enters down L and exits down R. She is followed seconds later by the King and Queen and several others. They mill around, then with loud whoops of glee exit in various directions

Carabosse disguised in a long, hooded cloak, enters down L

The Lights begin to fade to a green spot on Carabosse

Carabosse   The scene is set. My plans are made. Now let the fun begin.
                   Beneath my spell that fair princess will fall—and Carabosse
                   will *win*.

She casts a spell. There is a flash down L

Two Rats scurry on, carrying a small spinning wheel and a stool, which they place up C. The Rats exit

Carabosse sits at the spinning wheel and sets it in motion. The Lights have now dimmed to a green light surrounding Carabosse and the wheel

The Princess suddenly hurries on, glancing over her shoulder. She turns and sees Carabosse

Princess (*startled*) Oh. (*She comes to a halt near the wheel*) Who are *you*?
Carabosse   (*croaking*) Why, Bless my soul. I do declare it is the young
                   princess
                   I am the royal spinstress, dear, who spun the silk to make
                   your dress.
Princess (*strangely*) Spun? (*She smiles*) I'm sorry, but I don't know what
that means. Is it difficult?
Carbosse   Have you not seen my wheel spin out its endless shining
                   thread
                   That glistens like the golden (*raven/auburn*) hair upon
                   your pretty head?
Princess Why, no. I don't remember seeing anything like it before.
Carabosse   My child. You don't know what you've missed. Here, sit
                   upon my stool
                   And try *your* hand at spinning silk. (*She rises and moves
                   aside*)
Princess Oh, may I?
Carabosse   (*aside*) Little fool.

The Princess sits at the wheel and sets it in motion

                   (*To her*) Pedal, pedal, spin the wheel.
                   You're doing well, I vow. Now touch that little spindle
                   there. (*She points*)
Princess Is this it? (*Her finger hovers over the spindle*)
Carabosse Yes. Press *now*.

The Princess touches the spindle and pricks herself

Princess (*jumping up*) Oh. My finger. It's bleeding.

Everyone enters L *and* R. *They react to the scene*

King (*horrified*) Aurora.
Queen My little girl. (*She hurries towards her*)

Aurora's eyes close, and she falls to the ground. Everyone reacts. Carabosse throws back her hood

Carabosse   (*cackling*) The deed is done. The spell is cast,
              And sweet revenge is mine at last.

The Rats scurry back on and remove the wheel and stool

Fusspot Quickly. The royal couch. And summon the Princes.

Two Servants hurry out R

Carabosse No use. (*She cackles again*)
              Their kisses shall not waken her,
              I've been, you see, quite clever.
              She must be kissed by one *she* loves
              Or else she'll sleep forever. (*She draws herself upright*)
              So dies the hope your hearts did build.
              The curse I laid is now fulfilled.

With a great shriek of laughter, she swirls about and exits L

Tickles (*brokenly*) She's beaten us. We'll never be able to wake the princess now.
Dame How can she be woken by a prince she loves, when she's never had a chance *to* fall in love? (*She sobs*)
Shout Yes she has. She *did* do. In the garden this afternoon.
Queen (*startled*) Eh?

Two Servants enter with a silk covered bier

They place it up C, *and the King assists them to gently lift the sleeping princess on to it*

Bawl She told us about it. She thought she'd fallen in love with *him*.
Queen But that was just a dream.

Azuriel enters down R

Azuriel   A dream, and yet no dream at all, I'm happy to relate.
              The prince she loves, though not yet born, will live in
                some far distant date.
              One hundred years she'll sleep within this silent vaulted
                hall,
              Till 'gainst the mighty power of love, the spell of
                Carabosse shall fall.

All look dismayed

King (*moving down to them*) A hundred *years*?
Queen What use is *that* to us?

Dame I'll be nearly forty when she wakes up again.

Azuriel (*kindly*) Fear not. For all within this place
Shall sleep as she sleeps now,
And when she wakes, you'll all be there
To greet her. This I vow.

Fusspot But I can't afford to go to sleep for a hundred years. I've got to return my library books next week. Think of the fine I'd have to pay.

Tickles Don't worry, Chamberlain. I'll take 'em back for you.

Dame How can you, you fathead? You'll be asleep too.

Tickles No, I won't. I'm not going to snore my life away while that nasty old Carabosse woman's running about loose. I don't trust her. I'm going to use my time machine and travel into the future. That way I'll be able to make sure this Prince Valiant knows where the palace is, and nobody tries to stop him getting there.

Dame Here, what a smashing idea. I'll come with you.

Shout } (*together*) Us too.
Bawl }

Azuriel So be it, then, if that's your wish. But take great care, dear friends.
For more adventure lies in store before this story ends.

Tickles Don't worry, Missis Fairy. We can take care of ourselves. (*To the audience*) Cheerio, kids. See you in a hundred years' time.

Tickles, Dame, Shout and Bawl all exit R

Azuriel Come, sisters, weave your magic spells, bestow the gift of sleep;
Whilst round about this palace, tangled rose-briar shall its secret keep.

Fairies enter to graceful music and dance around the assembly

As they do so, King and Queen yawn and totter weakly to their thrones and sit, slowly slipping into sleep. Fusspot supports himself on his rod of office and his head sinks on to his chest. All other guests subside into a deep sleep. Through the open windows at the back, huge rose-briars are drawn up. More roses are lowered from above. At the end of the dance, all humans are sleeping silently and the Fairies stand in a triumphant attitude with Azuriel standing C

Sleep on, until that distant day
Prince Valiant here will make his way
This spell of Carabosse to break,
And Sleeping Beauty shall awake.

CURTAIN

ACT II

The village of Frolicking-in-the-forest. A hundred years later

A typical pantomime village setting with a backdrop of dense forest. Dame Goodbody's cottage is up L, *and has a practical door. Other shops and cottages are* L *and* R

When the CURTAIN *rises, Villagers are singing and dancing merrily on the village green. It is a bright and sunny day*

Song 8 (Villagers)

At the end of the song, Dame Goodbody enters from her cottage carrying a large notice. The words on it are hidden from the audience

Villagers (*brightly*) Good-morning, Dame Goodbody.
Dame (*moving down* C) Good-morning? Good-*morning*? What's so good about it? It's exactly the same sort of morning we've been having for the last ten years. Oooooh, I could *flatten* that Tickles.
Boy Whatever for?
Dame (*disgustedly*) Him and his time machine. Only brought us forward ninety years and then it broke down. We've been stuck here ever since and there hasn't been a sign of a prince from that day to this.
Girl (*bored*) Oh, not *that* old story again. We've heard it *so* often.
Boy Everyone *knows* it's impossible to travel through time.
Dame (*grimly*) Oh, yes? Well just let me catch you pinching my apples again, and you'll find out how wrong you are. I'll knock you into the middle of next week. Now clear off while I put this notification up somewhere.
Girl (*curious*) What does it say?

The Dame holds up the notice. It reads : WANTED—PRINCE VALIANT. APPLY WITHIN

Boy (*amused*) You don't really expect a prince to come visiting this place do you? There's nothing but forest for miles around.
Dame Oh, don't worry yourself, smarty-pants. He'll turn up all right. A hundred years ago, you couldn't move in these parts without tripping over a prince or two. (*She preens*) I was forever fighting them off.
Girl You? Fighting off princes? (*She looks amused*)
Dame Yes, me. I haven't always been thirty-two, you know. A hundred years ago I was an absolute *vision*.

Boy Yes. But now you're just a *sight*.

All laugh and exit

Dame (*fuming*) Ooooh. It's a good job I'm a lady of breeding and charm, otherwise I'd have smacked him one right in the kisser. (*She puts the notice down by the door*) Do you know, we've had nothing but trouble with that lot ever since the day we arrived. Mind you, I blame it all on Tickles. We hadn't been here a week before he went out and bought himself a great big tabby cat. (*To someone in the front rows*) Do you like cats, love? You do? (*She snorts*) Huh. You wouldn't like *this* one. It's the muckiest, scruffiest looking object you've ever seen in your life. And the *pong*. (*She winces*) Oooh. You can smell it in the custard on Sundays. Anyway, you won't believe this, but it took first prize in the local budgie show. *First prize*. It got into the cage and swallowed the winner. And tennis. Tennis. It's tennis mad. Watches it all the time. Still, I suppose it's only natural. Its mother's in the racket.

Tickles enters down R

Tickles (*brightly*) Hiya kids. (*To the Dame*) Hello, Ammonia.
Dame Never mind "Hello, Ammonia". Where do you think *you've* been all morning?
Tickles Oh, down at the church. I've been having a word with (*local vicar*).
Dame (*interested*) Ooooh. About our wedding? (*She looks excited*)
Tickles No, no. This is something important. I went to see him about something that was worrying me.
Dame What's that?
Tickles Well don't you remember last Sunday? When he told us it said in the Bible that everybody was made out of dust.
Dame Yes. Yes.
Tickles Well I don't see how that can be true. You see, if we're all made out of dust, why don't we get muddy when we have a bath?
Dame (*after a reaction*) You know, sunshine, you ought to get a job as a psychiatrist on a poultry farm.
Tickles (*baffled*) What for?
Dame You could look after the cracked eggs. (*Annoyed*) Listen, banana-brain, we've been here for ten years now, waiting for this Prince Valiant to come along. And what's happened, eh? I'll tell you. Nothing.
Tickles You can't blame *me* for that, Ammonia. I've been doing the best I could. I've been all round the world and several other places but I can't even find Euphoria, never mind Prince Valiant. I'd do a lot better if you came with me, you know.
Dame No fear. You're not getting *me* running round foreign countries again. Not after the last time. Oh, I was so embarrassed coming back through the Customs.
Tickles How's that?
Dame Well, you saw that young French girl in front of me? The blonde one who'd dyed her hair roots black. When the Customs officer opened *her* case, he found it filled with silk knickers. He said, "Here, here. What's all

this, then?" and she said, (*with a French accent*) "Oo-la-la. Monday, Tuesday, Wednesday, Thursday, Friday, Saturday, Sunday", and gave him a saucy wink. Then he opened *my* case, fished out my flannelette passion-killers and asked me why *I'd* got so many.

Tickles And what did you say?

Dame January, February, March, April—— (*She breaks off*) Anyway, never mind about that. What *I* want to know is how much longer I've got to wait before I get bridalized? We've been engaged for a hundred and fifteen years.

Tickles I know, but we don't want to *rush* things, do we? Besides, I'll have finished my new invention soon and then we'll be rich.

Dame New invention? I didn't know you were working on a new invention.

Tickles Oh, yes. It's going to make me a fortune. It's called colour television.

Dame Colour television? (*Scornfully*) Huh. I'll believe that when I see it in black and white.

Tickles Anyway, what have we got for lunch? I'm starving.

Dame You can have the slice of pie you didn't finish yesterday.

Tickles But I couldn't eat it. My teeth wouldn't go through the pastry. It was as tough as cardboard.

Dame I'm not surprised. You were chewing the paper plate. Anyway, that's all there is. We haven't a penny left in the world. If this Prince Valiant doesn't turn up today, we're done for. (*She looks miserable*)

Tickles Cheer up, Ammonia. Things could be worse.

Dame (*sniffling*) It's all right for you, but all this waiting around's putting years on *me*. I'm worried I might lose my looks as I get older. (*Anxiously*) Do *you* think I will?

Tickles (*reassuringly*) Oh, yes, if you're lucky. Now come on. Let's go into the cottage and have a nice cup of tea.

They exit into the cottage. As they do so, Azuriel enters down R

Azuriel   One hundred years have passed away. The time is drawing near

When Beauty shall awaken to embrace her prince most dear.

The tangled thorns that now conceal both kingdom and her bower,

Will vanish like the morning mist when love destroys that ancient power

And long-lost Entertainia from slumber can arise,

Once more its rightful place to take beneath the summer skies.

So to this place, by magic power, his footsteps I now guide;

That he may wake her with a kiss, and claim her as his bride.

Carabosse enters down L, *leaning on her stick*

Carabosse   You count your chicks, Azuriel, before they hatch, I fear.

This prince on whom you pin your hopes

Will also find *me* waiting here.
Despite your help, he'll never reach where Sleeping Beauty lies—
For should he make the *least* attempt, then death shall be his only prize.

Azuriel   (*pleading*) Dear Carabosse, I beg you, forget your cruel sport.
A century has now elapsed. Continuance avails you nought.
The child has done no harm to you. Repent and make amends.
Give unto her your blessing, and let us once more be friends.

Carabosse   (*coldly*) You plead in vain, Azuriel, for whilst I still draw breath
My only aim in life shall be to celebrate her death.

Azuriel   So be it. From this moment on, as deadly foes we'll meet.
Prince Valiant his bride *shall* win, and *you* experience defeat.

Azuriel exits

Carabosse   (*darkly*) Defeat? Oh, no, Azuriel. Your prince shall find no wife.
He'll not forswear my vengeance, for he too shall lose his life.
In yonder forest's darkest depths wherein the palace lies,
I'll wait for his arrival, then I give my word—he *dies*.

Carabosse exits

Shout and Bawl enter down R

Bawl (*wearily*) Oooh, I'm shattered. We must have walked twenty miles this morning. I wish we had some money. I could just do with a pint of beer.

Shout Not me. You wouldn't catch me drinking that stuff. It's very bad for you, beer is.

Bawl Don't be daft. I have a pint of beer every day. What's bad about it?

Shout I was watching this demonstration last week. A man took a pint of beer and dropped a great big juicy worm into it, and the poor thing just sank to the bottom, turned its tail up, and kicked the bucket.

Bawl Kicked the bucket? You mean, it *died*? This worm?

Shout That's right. Dead within minutes. Now what does *that* prove, eh?

Bawl thinks

Bawl If ever you get worms, drink beer.

Prince Valiant enters up R

Prince (*seeing them*) Excuse me. (*He moves down to them*) Would you mind telling me where I am?

Shout and Bawl exchange glances

Bawl You're right there. (*He indicates*)
Prince (*amused*) No, no. I mean, what's the name of this village?

Shout Oh. It's called Frolicking-in-the-forest.

Prince (*frowning*) I see. (*Indicating off* L) And where does that road lead one to?

Bawl Well, it's led quite a few people round here into *trouble*.

Shout (*pushing him*) Shut up. (*To the Prince*) What's the matter? Are you lost or something?

Prince (*ruefully*) I'm afraid so. I was riding at the edge of the forest over there, when suddenly my horse threw me and ran away. I hadn't a hope of catching him.

Bawl Oh, *I* know a way of stopping a runaway horse, just like that. (*He snaps his finger and thumb*)

Prince How?

Bawl Place a bet on it. It never fails.

Shout hits him

Owww.

Shout (*to the prince*) So you're a stranger round here, are you?

Prince Yes. I'm from a country many miles away. At least a year's journey.

Bawl And are you on a pleasure trip, or is your wife with you?

Shout glares at him and he quickly backs away

Prince (*smiling*) As a matter of fact, I'm travelling from country to country just searching for the girl of my dreams.

Shout Well you won't find her in this place, I can tell you. Not unless you've been having some very funny dreams. What sort of girl are you looking for, anyway?

Prince (*dreamily*) The most beautiful girl in the world. Isn't that what every man wants?

Bawl Not us. Beautiful girls have never bothered us.

Shout No. (*Regretfully*) But we wish they would.

Prince (*looking around*) What a fascinating place. If you'll forgive my saying so, it's the quaintest little village I've ever come across.

Shout Yes, it is a bit old fashioned. Even the television sets are run on gas.

Prince Still, with all this fresh air, I expect everyone is healthy.

Bawl Not half. If ever they want to start a cemetery here, they'll have to kill somebody.

Prince I am—er—I don't suppose there's anywhere I can stay until my horse is found, is there?

Shout You could always try (*names local hotel*) but it's a bit on the posh side. If you ask for fresh milk to put on your cornflakes, they bring a cow into the dining-room.

Prince But are the rooms quiet?

Bawl Oh, yes. It's the people inside them that make all the noise.

Prince Well, thank you for your kindness. Here's a gold piece. (*He gives them a coin from the pouch at his waist*)

Shout (*gazing at it*) Cor, money. (*To Bawl*) Quick. Let's show it to Dame Goodbody. Looks like we'll be eating today after all.

They exit into the cottage delightedly

Prince (*sighing deeply*) Is it all a waste of time? Should I return to Euphoria and admit it was only a dream? (*With sudden resolution*) No. I couldn't have imagined it. It was *much* too real. Even after I woke, I could still smell her perfume, and her face has haunted me ever since. Entertainia *does* exist. I know it. Somewhere on earth it lays hidden and, inside the royal palace, Princess Aurora is still sleeping, just as the legend says. I'll find her if it's the last thing I do. As my old nurse used to say, "If you don't try, how can you ever succeed?" and she never spoke a truer word.

Song 9 (Prince)

At the end of the song, he turns and sees the notice by the cottage door

(*Surprised*) What's this? (*Reading*) "Wanted—Prince Valiant. Apply within." (*Amazed*) But that's incredible. No-one here could possibly have heard of me. What can it mean?

The cottage door flies open and Shout and Bawl hurry out, followed by Tickles and Dame Goodbody

Shout (*indicating the Prince*) There he is. That's him.
Dame Quick, surround him. Don't let him get away.

They encircle the Prince

Prince (*bewildered*) What's wrong? Who are you?
Bawl Never mind who *we* are. Who are *you*?
Dame And where did you get that gold piece from? The one you gave these two. (*She indicates Shout and Bawl*)
Prince Was something wrong with it?
Tickles No. Only with the words stamped on it. The Royal Treasury of Euphoria.
Prince But that's the country I come from. All our coins say that.
Dame *What?* (*She peers at him*) Here, you wouldn't happen to be a certain Prince Valiant, would you?
Prince Why yes. But how did *you* know?
Dame (*bursting into tears of joy*) It's him. It's him. He's arrived at last.
Prince (*baffled*) Arrived? I don't understand. How could you know I even existed?
Shout The princess told us. Princess Aurora.
Prince (*startled*) What?
Bawl Before she pricked her finger on the spindle.
Tickles She dreamed she'd met you in the palace gardens and you'd fallen in love.
Prince (*dazed*) I must be hearing things.
Dame (*sniffling*) It was the day of her sixteenth birthday.
Prince Then it *wasn't* a dream. I really *did* meet her. But—but how could I have done? And how could you have spoken to her? Entertainia vanished from human sight a hundred years ago. It's only a legend, now.
Tickles Oh, no it isn't. It's hidden in the middle of that forest, and we've

come here in my time machine to lead you to it. According to the Fairy Azuriel, you're the only one who can break the spell and wake everybody up again. It has to be done by somebody the princess loves, you see.

Prince But ... how do I do it?

Dame By giving her the kiss of life. (*Suddenly alert*) Here, I don't suppose you'd like to get a bit of practice in with *me*, would you? (*She puckers her lips and flutters her eyelashes at him*)

Tickles (*warningly*) Ammonia.

Dame (*making a face*) Yes, you're probably right. I shouldn't kiss a feller who wears fish-net tights and high heels. I might smudge his lipstick.

Prince (*dazedly*) I can hardly believe it. For two years I've been searching for the lost kingdom, all the time trying to convince myself I hadn't fallen in love with a figment of my imagination. Then just as I'd almost given up in despair, you all appear and give me fresh hope. Who says dreams can't come true?

Dame Well it's certainly not me. Because once you've woken the princess and everything's back to normal, there's going to be the biggest wedding ever seen in Entertainia.

Prince Oh, I don't know about that. I think *I'd* prefer a quiet one with just a few special friends.

Dame Well you can have what you want. I'm talking about *mine*. Tickles has promised to marry me on the very same day. Oh, I can just see myself sweeping down the aisle in my drip-dry wedding dress. Everybody singing "Here Comes the Bride". (*She flutters*)

Tickles Yes. And the organ playing "Here We Are Again".

Dame (*to the Prince*) I've been saving myself for him since the middle of last century, you know.

Tickles Yes. But I wish she hadn't saved so much.

Prince Well I hope you'll be very happy, but just for the moment I'd like to get to Entertainia as quickly as possible. If I *am* going to wake the princess, I don't want to keep her waiting a moment longer than I have to.

Shout Right. This way, Mr Prince. Follow us.

Bawl To the royal palace of Entertainia.

With much excitement they all exit

Quick fade to Black-out

SCENE 2

A footpath in the forest

Carabosse enters L

Carabosse   It seems that once again my warnings fall on stony
                  ground:
                  Azuriel has called the prince, and now he's hither bound.
                  (*Waspishly*) O foolish prince to thus incur the wrath of
                  Carabosse.

Your bones shall bleach within this place, and none shall
mourn your loss.
You'll never wake that sleeping maid, I give you promise
fair.
Although the palace you may find, just enter if you *dare*.

She cackles with laughter and stamps out. As she does so, Tickles enters R,
followed by the Dame, Prince, Shout and Bawl. Bawl is limping

Tickles (*wearily*) Hiya, kids. (*To the others*) Come on, everybody. We must
be almost there.

Bawl (*groaning*) Oooh, I can't walk another step. I've got a great big blister
on my foot.

Dame Well walk on your other one, then.

Shout Cheer up, Bawl. As soon as we get to the palace, you can soak your
feet in some nice hot water.

Bawl What? And get my shoes wet?

Prince Are you sure we're going in the right direction, Tickles? We do seem
to have been walking for some hours.

Tickles Don't worry. I know exactly where we are. I recognize that twisted
old tree over there. (*He indicates*)

Dame I'm not surprised. We've passed it five times already. (*Annoyed*)
We're lost, aren't we? Absolutely lost.

Tickles Of course we're not. How can we be lost when we're all here? It's the
palace that's lost. Anyway, there's nothing to get excited about. You're
looking at one of the world's greatest trackers. I can find my way
anywhere, I can. I used to be a big-game hunter before I became a jester,
you know.

Shout (*impressed*) Cor. Have you ever hunted bear?

Tickles No. But I've gone fishing in my underpants.

Bawl (*groaning*) Oooh, I wonder what time it is? It must be time we had
something to eat.

Dame Yes. I must admit *I'm* feeling a bit on the peckish side. Perhaps we
should stop for lunch. What time *is* it?

Shout Hang on a second, and I'll tell you. Where's the sun? (*He looks up*)

Prince (*impressed*) Do you mean to say you can use the sun to help you tell
the time?

Shout Oh, yes. Nothing simpler. Ah, there it is.

Prince How do you do it?

Shout Well, you just find out where the sun is, shade your eyes like *this*, (*he
shades his eyes with one hand*) then look at your wrist watch. (*He does so*)
It's half-past twelve.

Bawl hits him

Dame Oh, stop messing about. We're never going to find the palace at this
rate. Look, I think we'd better split up. Me and Tickles'll go that way (*she
indicates* L) and you go back the way we came and see if you can find
another path.

Bawl What shall we do if we *do* find one?

Tickles Make a big mark in the mud, then come back and tell us.

Shout But what happens if *you* find it *first*?

Dame Oh, you do ask some daft questions. We'll rub the mark out, of course. Now come on. Let's get going.

Prince (*tiredly*) It's no use. The trees are growing so close together now, there's hardly room to squeeze past. And look at those briars ahead. They're like a wall of thorns. We'll never be able to get through those.

Shout Perhaps we could burn a way through?

Tickles How can we? We've got nothing to light a fire with.

Bawl Ah, now that's where you're wrong. Me and Shout used to be Boy Scouts and *we* know how to start a fire by using just two little sticks.

Tickles How do you do that?

Dame By making sure that *one* of those two sticks is a *match*. (*Annoyed*) Oooh, you Higgorant Herald. Hasn't anybody ever told you never to light a fire in a forest? You could burn the whole place down.

Prince Dame Goodbody's right. (*He sighs*) If only we had a *sword* or something. Perhaps we could chop our way through?

Azuriel enters R

All react

Who are *you*?

Tickles (*excitedly*) It's Azuriel. The fairy we told you about. She's come to help us.

Azuriel   Rejoice, young prince. Your quest soon ends. I'll lead you
                 to the bower
                 Wherein the Sleeping Beauty lies. Her face you'll see
                 within the hour.
                 But first your wish I mean to grant. Upon you I bestow
                 The sword of Good King Arthur, that all evil can
                 o'er-throw.

She waves her wand and a huge mailed fist appears from behind the procenium arch, the great sword Excalibur held firmly in its grasp

Tickles Oooh, look. A stage hand. (*Loudly*) By the power of Numbskull.

Dame (*pushing him*) Oh, shut up.

The Prince crosses to the sword and takes it. The hand withdraws

Prince I thank you, good fairy, but will I need a sword as powerful as Excalibur simply to cut through forest thorns?

Azuriel   (*shaking her head*) No blade you'll need to clear your way,
                 By secret paths I'll guide you;
                 But though success seems near,
                 Keep great Excalibur beside you.
                 For Carabosse has vowed to take your life this very day
                 And lest you keep a watchful eye, indeed, I fear, she may.
                 That mighty sword is all she fears, so wield it with good
                 heart

Should you have cause to do so. Now come. We must
depart.

With a flourish of her wand she exits R, *followed by Tickles, Dame, Shout
and Bawl*

Prince Valiant remains C

Prince (*gazing at the sword in wonder*) The sword of King Arthur. And in
my hands. It's past all belief. Only this morning I was in despair—and
now I'm on my way to the lost Kingdom of Entertainia to awaken my
future bride. Well, Carabosse or no Carabosse, there's nothing going to
stop me now.

Song 10 (Prince)

At the end of the song, he hurries off R

The Lights fade quickly to Black-out

SCENE 3

The great ballroom of the royal palace

*The set is identical to Act I, Scene 5 except that all flags and decorations, etc.,
are ragged and dusty. Everyone is in a cobwebby condition and placed exactly
as they were at the end of that scene*

Carabosse enter L *and moves* C

Carabosse   Speed swiftly to this palace, gallant prince, so soon to
perish.
My little gift you'll find when you approach the one you
cherish.
Alas, your lips will never touch that maiden pure and
sweet.
Instead you'll rest forever in the dust beneath her feet.

She gives a triumphant cackle and exits L. *As she does so, enter Tickles,
Dame, Shout and Bawl. They look around with amazement as they move
down* L

Tickles (*in a soft voice*) Hiya, kids.
Shout Cor, isn't it eerie? (*He peers at Fusspot closely*)
Bawl Looks like a meeting of (*local Town Council*).
Dame Ooh look at all this dust. We'll have to get that cleaned up before
tonight.
Tickles Yes. Here, and I've got the very thing to do it. My latest invention.
A vacuum cleaner that's so good it'll do half the work for us.
Dame In that case, we'd better have two. (*She looks around*) Where's Prince
Valiant got to?
Shout (*looking off* R) Here he comes now.

The Prince enters R, *his sword in a scabbard*

Prince (*awed*) It's absolutely amazing. If Azuriel hadn't led us here, we'd never have found it. (*He sees the Princess*) The Princess. (*He hurries to the bier and looks down at her*) How beautiful she is. Exactly as I saw her in my dream. And now to waken her.

He stoops to kiss her. A loud hissing noise comes from behind the bier and a huge snake rises into view. The Prince staggers back as the snake menaces him. Shout and Bawl dash down L, and Tickles jumps into the Dame's arms with a shriek of fright

(*To them*) Keep back. I'll deal with it.

He draws his sword and does battle with the snake until he manages to kill it. All cheer as it falls back behind the bier

    Carabosse enters in a fury

Carabosse   A curse upon you, Valiant. You were not fighting fair.
    No man-made sword could kill the beast you slaughtered
       over there.
    You'll rue the day you crossed my path to set these
       sleepers free,
    For though it seems you've come out best, you have not
       seen the last of me.
Prince (*raising his sword to her*) Begone, you old harridan, or I'll give you a taste of your own medicine. (*He advances on her*)

    Carabosse gives a shriek of fright and quickly exits

The Prince sheaths his sword and moves back to the bier. He lightly kisses the Princess, then steps back

Tickles (*anxiously*) Is anything happening?
Prince (*puzzled*) Not a thing.
Dame (*worried*) Perhaps you didn't kiss her hard enough.

Everyone moves closer to the bier

Oh, I knew I should have given you some lessons before we arrived here. The last man *I* kissed almost went up in flames.
Tickles Well what did you expect? You still had your cigarette in your mouth when you did it.

The Dame glowers at him

Bawl Look. She's starting to move.

All cluster round the bier, eagerly

Shout (*delightedly*) He's done it. She's waking up.

The Princess gives a deep sigh and opens her eyes

Princess Where am I? (*She sees the Prince*) Prince Valiant. (*She sits up*)
Prince (*bowing deeply*) Welcome to the seventeenth century, Your Highness.

Princess (*bewildered*) I don't understand. (*She looks around*) What's wrong
with everyone? (*She gets off the bier*) Mother—Father.
Dame (*quickly*) There's nothing to worry about, dear. They're just having
forty winks. They'll be waking up in a minute.
Princess (*anxiously*) But what's happened to them? And why does every-
thing look so dirty?
Tickles (*soothingly*) There, there, Princess. We'll explain everything to you.
Just come into the garden and we'll tell you exactly what's been going on.
Bawl Yes. It'll do you good to get a breath of fresh air, and you can see all
the little flowers that have grown up without anybody helping them.
Shout (*puzzled*) What sort of flowers are *they*?
Bawl Self-raising flowers.

*Shout hits him with his cap and the Prince leads the Princess, Dame and
Tickles out L. Shout and Bawl follow, grousing at each other. As they exit,
Azuriel enters down R*

Azuriel   The Sleeping Beauty wakes at last, and soon shall be a
                         wife.
                     So now, as promised years ago, the royal court returns to
                         life.
                     Once more its corridors and halls shall ring with joyous
                         laughter,
                     And all within live happily for now and ever after.

Azuriel waves her wand and exits R

*The Court with the exception of the King, Queen and Fusspot, begins to stir.
The rose briars fall from the outside of the windows, and the overhead briars
are raised out of sight. The room brightens as daylight pours into it. Fusspot
lets out a great snore. Startled, the Queen wakes and she takes in the scene*

Queen (*startled*) Aaaaagh. (*She grabs the King and shakes him*) Cedric.
Cedric.
King (*drowsily*) Hmm? Hmm? What's the matter?
Queen The spell. It's broken. We're all waking up.
King (*tiredly*) Don't be silly, dear. You must be dreaming. Go back to sleep.

By now people are standing and gazing round in astonishment

Queen (*shaking the King again*) Cedric. It's morning.
King Yes, dear. (*His eyes open wide*) Morning? (*He sits up*) Morning.
(*Delightedly*) Morning. (*To the Queen*) Semmi, dear, why didn't you *tell*
me? (*He jumps to his feet*) Wake up, everyone. It's morning.

Another loud snore comes from Fusspot

Fusspot. Fusspot.

Everyone smiles or giggles as he slumbers on

(*Loudly*) Fusspot. Wake up.

Fusspot slumbers on

Queen (*gently*) Let me try, dear. (*She rises*) Oh, thank goodness it's *payday*.
Fusspot (*wakening with a start*) Payday? Payday? (*His hand shoots out*)

Everyone laughs. Fusspot gazes around in astonishment

King Quickly, everyone. Gather round.

All move closer

> If the spell's broken, we must have been asleep for a hundred years. That
> means, at any time now, this mysterious prince is going to arrive and
> waken our darling Aurora. So what I want you to do is——
Fusspot (*pointing at the empty bier*) Aaaaaaaah.

Everyone is startled

King (*twitching*) What is it? What's wrong?
Fusspot The princess, sire. She's gone.

Everyone looks and reacts

Queen (*anguished*) He's right. Cedric, she's been kidnapped.
King (*to Fusspot*) Quick. Quick. Run out and call the guards.
Fusspot No, no, sire. Wait. (*He stoops over in thought*)
King What is it Fusspot? And why are you standing like that?
Fusspot I've got a hunch, sire.
King After sleeping in *that* position for a hundred years, I'm not surprised.
  I've got a bit of back-ache, myself.
Fusspot No, no, sire. I mean, I have an idea. Perhaps we've overslept.
Queen Overslept?
Fusspot Yes, Your Majesty. Maybe the prince has been and gone, taking
  the princess with him.
Queen And leaving *us* all here? Oh, they wouldn't do that to us. (*To the
  King; doubtfully*) Would they?
King I don't know, dear. If we *have* overslept, we could have been here for
  centuries. It could even be (*current year*) for all *we* know.

All gasp with dismay

Queen Well, there's one way to find out, isn't there?
Fusspot What's that, Your Majesty?
Queen Tell one of the footmen to find the nearest railway line and lie down
  in the middle of the tracks.
King But what good would *that* do, Semmi? The first train to come along
  would run right over him.
Queen I know dear. But if he starves to death before it arrives, it'll *prove*
  we're in (*current year*).

Tickles enters up L

Tickles Your Majesties. Everybody. Welcome back to life.

All greet him

King (*delightedly*) Tickles. My faithful Court Jester. (*He shakes hands*)

Queen Oh, we're so glad to see you. But where are the others? And what's happened to our darling Aurora?

Tickles (*brightly*) It's all right, Your Majesty. They're all out in the garden. The princess as well.

King You mean he actually arrived? The prince. And woke her up?

Queen (*eagerly*) Oh, I can't wait to meet him. Quick, Fussie. Go out and tell them we're back to normal.

Fusspot (*excitedly*) At once, Your Majesty.

Fusspot scurries out up L

Queen (*suddenly dismayed*) Oh, but wait. We can't greet him looking like this. Everyone find something *decent* to wear.

Tickles Oh, you don't have to worry about clothes, Your Majesty. This is sixteen sixty-two. Everything's modern. Folk wear anything they like, these days.

Queen Perhaps they do, but I'm not having visitors seeing us dressed in rags. Quickly, everyone. Into your Sunday clothes.

Song 11 (Queen and Ensemble)

At the end of the song, all Choristers exit quickly

King I suppose *I'd* better try and find something respectable, too. (*He thinks*) How about my purple and orange suit with the lime-green stripes and day-glow scarlet fleur-de-lis?

Queen (*dismayed*) Oh, no, Cedric. You can't possibly wear that drab old thing. Wear something bright and cheerful. (*Shaking her head*) I think *I'll* have to start picking your clothes in future. I'm quite good at it.

King Yes. You've been picking my *pockets* for years. (*To Tickles*) Tell me, Tickles, has the world changed a lot since we went to sleep?

Tickles Oh, yes, Your Majesty. It's a whole different place now. You remember at one time, everyone thought the world was *flat*.

King Yes, of course. But *then* we decided that it really was *round*.

Tickles True. Well nowadays, most people know that half of it's *crooked*.

The Princess, Prince, Dame, Shout, Bawl and Fusspot enter

Princess (*delightedly*) Mother. Father. (*She hurries to embrace them*)

Queen Aurora. My little girl. (*She hugs her*)

King My precious. (*He kisses her*)

Dame (*to the audience*) Ooooh. (*She thumps her heart*) It gets you right here, doesn't it?

Queen Thank goodness we're all together again.

Princess (*indicating the Prince*) And this is Prince Valiant. The one who broke the spell.

Prince (*bowing deeply*) Your Majesties.

King (*overcome*) My dear boy. However can we thank you enough?

Prince Your royal happiness is my reward, sire; but as your kingdom and daughter are now restored to you, may I ask for Aurora's hand in marriage?

Queen Oh, you can have *all* of her.

King (*after a wince*) Of course. And you'll have the most splendid wedding we can afford—even if we have to pawn the Crown Jewels to pay for it.

Prince (*laughing*) You don't have to worry about money, Your Majesty. I've got so much, I don't know what to do with it all. From now on, you'll have money to burn.

Everyone looks delighted

Dame (*giving a discreet cough*) Ahem. If you don't mind my saying so, I think we should leave these two love-birds alone for a while.

Shout (*blankly*) What for?

Dame Well, to give them a chance to get to know each other a bit better. (*Simpering*) I was a teenager myself, once, you know.

Bawl Blimey. What a memory she's got.

Fusspot I agree with Dame Goodbody. And besides, if we *are* going to have a royal wedding, there's a thousand and one things to do before the great day.

King Indeed there is, Fusspot. Come along, everyone. We'll go and discuss them, and have tea in the royal chambers.

Tickles (*pulling a face*) Oooh, we've not run out of cups, have we?

The Dame hits him, then all but Prince and Princess exit R

Princess (*turning to the Prince*) Oh, Valiant, I can hardly believe it. You're exactly as I remember seeing you on my birthday.

Prince And you're the very image of my dream. If you ask me, I think Azuriel had something to do with our meeting.

Princess (*in wonderment*) To think I've had a fairy godmother all my life, and never even knew about it. We *must* thank her for all she's done to help us.

Prince We shall. She'll be guest of honour at our wedding. But just for now, all I want to do is celebrate your awakening and tell the whole world how happy I am.

Song 12 (Prince and Princess)

At the end of the song, a loud cry for help is heard off R

Princess (*alarmed*) Valiant. Someone's in trouble.

Prince Wait here. I'll go see what's happening.

The Prince draws his sword and hurries out R. There is a flash and Carabosse enters down L

Princess (*startled*) Oh. (*Recognizing her*) You. (*She turns to run*) Valiant.

Carabosse Hold fast.

She casts a spell and the Princess halts

Your prince can't help you now. You're snared within my net
Despite his interference, my revenge I'll have e'en yet.

She grabs hold of the Princess's arm

Princess (*struggling*) Let go of me. Let go.
Carabosse   Oh, no. This time you shan't escape. Of that, you may be
                certain.
                You'll die before this day is out. Come, face your final
                curtain.
Princess No. (*Calling loudly*) Help. Help.

Carabosse drags her off down L. *A moment later, Prince Valiant enters* R

Prince (*puzzled*) That's strange. I couldn't see anyone at—— (*He looks
around*) Aurora? Aurora, where are you?

There is a scream off L, *followed by a cackle of laughter from Carabosse*

(*Alarmed*) Aurora?

*The King and Queen hurry on, followed by Fusspot, Shout, Bawl and the
Chorus*

King What was that?
Queen Who screamed?
Chorus What's happening? (*Etc. etc.*)
Prince It's Aurora. She's been kidnapped by Carabosse.

*There is a big reaction. The King faints in the Queen's arms. Fusspot hurriedly
fans him. The chorus are very upset and there is general despair*

Black-out

SCENE 4

An ante-room in the palace

Tickles enters R

Tickles (*softly*) Hiya, kids. Shhhhh. I don't want Ammonia to know I'm
here. If she finds out I'm here talking to you, she'll start going on again
about *us* getting married. Here, isn't it exciting, though? Everything back
to normal and the princess and that Prince Valiant having a royal
wedding. Oooh, I love weddings, don't you? Mind you, you meet some
very funny people there. The last one *I* went to, there was this very snooty
looking woman sitting next to me, and I said to her "Excuse me, missis,
but are you a friend of the groom, too?" She said "Certainly *not*. I'm the
bride's mother."

The Dame enters L, *in a hurry*

Dame (*reeling*) Oh, Tickles. Tickles. (*She clutches at the proscenium arch for
support*)
Tickles (*looking round*) Oh ... Hello, Ammonia.
Dame (*clutching at her heart*) It's the princess. The princess.
Tickles (*disbelievingly*) Oh, give over. You don't look a bit like the princess.

Dame (*recovering*) No, no, you fathead. She's just been cat-napped—I mean kidnapped. That nasty old Carabosse has just flown off into the woods with her. (*Bursting into tears*) Oh, whatever shall we do?

Tickles (*striking a heroic pose*) Don't worry, Ammonia. *I'll* rescue her.

Dame (*startled*) You?

Tickles Yes. Don't you remember? I was the one who found that tall thin burglar who hit the king in the face, one night in the garden.

Dame (*remembering*) Oh, yes. *You* trod on the rake as well, didn't you? (*Annoyed*) How can you rescue her when we don't even know where she is, you two-toned twerp?

Tickles Simple. We ask Azuriel to *tell* us where she is.

Dame And how do we get in contact with her, pray? Stick an advert in (*local paper*)?

Tickles Why not? It only costs ten pounds an inch.

Dame (*amazed*) Ten pounds an inch? We can't afford *that*. She must be five feet tall.

Azuriel enters R

Azuriel   Dear friends, I hear your summons and by virtue of my power
                     Will lead you, and Prince Valiant, to Carabosse's bower.
                     Within the forest deep she dwells. The princess you'll find there,
                     And all will turn out happily—providing you take care.
                     It's time that someone put a stop to Carabosse's plan,
                     And with my help, I hereby vow, Prince Valiant shall be the man.

Dame Just give me five minutes to get my cast iron frying pan. I'll smack her so hard in the face with it, she'll be breathing out of the back of her head for a fortnight.

Azuriel   Then come. Let's find our champion. No further delay.
                     The final battle must be fought before we see the end of day.

Azuriel waves her wand and exits R, *followed by Dame and Tickles. As they go, Shout and Bawl enter* L

Shout Here, where are *they* going?

Bawl I don't know. Perhaps we'd better follow them.

Shout No fear. They could be going miles. And you know what I'm like. I always start feeling sick on the day of a long journey.

Bawl Well that's your own fault. You should set off on the day before.

Shout (*disgustedly*) Has anyone told you how stupid you are?

Bawl Here, who are you calling stupid? I've got brains I haven't ever used yet.

Shout Oh yes? Well what do you know about Sigmund Freud, then?

Bawl (*blankly*) Sigmund who?

Shout Freud. Freud. You see? You've never heard of him, have you?

Bawl No. But I know his brother, French Freud.

Shout (*tiredly*) Oooh, I don't know why I put up with you. There's nothing inside that head of yours but a vacuum.
Bawl Oh, no? Well what about my photographic memory, then?
Shout Photographic memory? You haven't got a photographic memory.
Bawl Yes, I have.
Shout Well in that case, it's a pity you've never had it developed. You'd forget your own head if it was loose.
Bawl Is that so? Well for your information, my memory is so marvellous, there's only three things I *can't* remember. One of them is names, and the other one is faces.
Shout That's only *two*. What's the third thing.
Bawl I've forgotten.

Song 13 (Shout and Bawl)

At the end of the song they exit quickly

Black-out

SCENE 5

Outside the cottage of Carabosse

A gloomy clearing in the forest. Carabosse's cottage, half-hidden in shadow, is up L. *It has a practical door*

When the Lights come up, Huntsmen are performing a spirited dance. Other Choristers and Babes are dressed as Game, and dart about in fright as the dance progresses

Dance (Huntsmen and Game)

At the end of the dance, all exit. Carabosse enters L, *dragging the Princess behind her*

Princess Let go of me. Let go. (*Calling over her shoulder*) Valiant. Help.
Carabosse   In vain you call. Your time, my dear, alas, is running out.
                  No help you'll get from anyone, however loud you shout.
                  And now inside my cottage whilst I plan your mode of
                     death.
                  Within the hour, at long last, you'll draw your final
                     breath.
Princess (*afraid*) No.

Carabosse swings the Princess round and propels her into the cottage, closing the door behind them

A moment later, Prince Valiant appears down R, *sword in hand. He looks round cautiously*

Prince So this is where Carabosse lives. What a gloomy looking place. No wonder she's so bad tempered. I'll look through the window and see if they're hidden inside. (*He crosses stealthily to the cottage and attempts to look inside*) No use. It's so dirty, I can't see anything. Perhaps I'll have better luck round the back.

He moves round the back of the cottage, vanishing from sight. As he does so, Tickles and the Dame enter down R

Tickles (*cheerily*) Hiya kids.

Dame (*pushing him*) Shhhhh, you fathead. We don't want old Carabosse knowing we've arrived to rescue the princess.

Tickles (*realizing*) Sorry, Ammonia. I wasn't thinking. My mind was wandering, you see.

Dame Well don't let it wander. It's too weak to be out on its own.

Tickles (*surprised*) Eh?

Dame (*annoyed*) Honestly. Fancy walking out here and screaming "Hiya, kids" at the top of your voice. Oooh, you're so stupid at times.

Tickles No, I'm not. (*To the audience*) Am I, kids?

Dame (*pulling him back*) You see? You see? You're doing it again. (*To the audience*) Don't encourage him. He's so stupid, he still thinks Pontius Pilot works for British Airways.

Tickles Well, I might not be as clever as *some* people, but I've always managed to keep my head above water.

Dame Yes, but only because wood floats. Now come on. Stop messing about and let's see if we can find that Prince Valiant. He must be round here, somewhere. (*She moves towards the cottage*)

Tickles Eh? You what?

Dame (*heavily*) I said let's go see if we can find the prince. Why don't you pay a little attention?

Tickles I'm paying as little as I can. (*Put out*) Besides, I don't know that I want to go looking for him. Not with *you*, anyway.

Dame Why not? (*She moves back to him*)

Tickles Because you've done nothing but moan at me ever since we left the palace, and I'm fed up of it.

Dame (*contritely*) Oh, I'm sorry Tickles. It's just that my nerves are all on edge. I'm so worried about Aurora.

Tickles (*generously*) Oh, you don't have to worry, Ammonia. We'll save her in time. That Carabosse doesn't stand a chance against *us*.

Dame What makes you think that?

Tickles Well, let's just say it's because of my *army* background.

Dame Army background? You've never been in the army in your life.

Tickles I know I haven't, but I come from a military *family*. (*Proudly*) In fact one of my ancestors fell at Waterloo.

Dame Yes. Somebody pushed him off platform seven.

Fusspot (*off,* R) Coo-ee. Is anybody there?

Fusspot enters

(*Seeing them*) Oh, thank goodness we've found you. (*Calling off* R) Here they are, Your Majesties. Outside this little cottage.

Dame }
Tickles } (*together*) Shhhhhhhh.

Dame (*hissing*) What are *you* doing here?

Fusspot We've been following you for *miles*. Their majesties are quite worn out.

The King and Queen enter wearily R

King (*groaning*) Ooooh. Quick. Get me a chair. I've got to have a sit down.

Tickles You can't sit down here, Your Majesty. We're right outside the place where Carabosse lives. (*He indicates*)

Queen Oh, isn't it quaint? Just like a chocolate box.

King Quaint? Quaint? It's an absolute disgrace, dear. That's the old gamekeeper's cottage. It should have been knocked down years ago.

Queen (*surprised*) Whatever for?

King Well, it shouldn't have been built there in the first place. There's the gas-works to the north of it, the rubber factory to the south. The sewage farm to the east and the glue factory to the west. It's in a *terrible* position. Nothing to recommend it at all.

Queen Oh, I don't know, Cedric. At least she'll always be able to tell which way the wind's blowing.

Dame Never mind about that, Your Majesties. You've got to get away from here. If Carabosse comes out and sees you, there's no knowing what she'll do.

Fusspot (*worried*) Dame Goodbody's right, Your Majesty. She could turn ugly.

King Well she's no oil painting now. No. I'm not leaving here till my daughter's been rescued, even if I've got to do it myself.

Dame But——

King (*firmly*) Silence. My Majesty has spoken. (*He looks around*) Now where's that Prince Valiant?

Tickles (*aside to the Dame*) It's all right, Ammonia. I'll get rid of them. Listen to this. (*To the others*) Well, *you* can stay if you like, but *I'm* going back to the palace. I don't like haunted places.

Queen (*startled*) Haunted?

Tickles That's right. This place is supposed to be haunted by a ghost that's so dreadful, anybody that sees it goes mad and has to be locked up in a special building with all the other mad people.

Queen You mean they're put in the House of Commons? (*Her fingers go to her mouth in horror*)

King (*trying to be brave*) Oh, don't talk such nonsense, Tickles. There's no such thing as ghosts.

Tickles Oh, yes there are. (*To the audience*) Aren't there, kids? (*He gives them a big wink*)

Audience reaction

(*To the King, Queen and Fusspot*) You see? Well, I'll be off now. Cheerio. (*To the Dame quietly*) I'll be back in a minute.

Tickles exits

Fusspot (*nervously*) Oh, dear. Suddenly it *does* feel rather haunted here.

Dame Never mind, Fussie. I'm sure a big strong man like you isn't afraid of a silly old ghost.

Fusspot Eh? Oh . . . No. No, indeed, Dame Goodbody. As a matter of fact, I know exactly what steps to take should a ghost come along—great big long ones.

Dame Oh, ghosts won't hurt you if you sing, you know. They don't like music. It drives them away.

Fusspot (*interested*) Does it really? Well, in that case, why don't we all sing and then we'll know we're not in any danger?

Queen What a good idea. And the boys and girls can warn us if anything *does* come creeping round. (*To the audience*) Will you do that for Queenie, boys and girls?

Audience reaction

Oh, good. (*To the others*) Now what shall we sing?

King I know. "She was only a cowboy's daughter, but she had the best calves in the West."

Fusspot Or how about "Get out the sausages, Granny, we're coming to a fork in the road"?

Dame No, no. Let's keep it simple. We'll sing "Nellie Dean". We all know *that*, don't we?

They begin to sing

Tickles creeps on covered in a white sheet

He moves to the Dame, raises the edge of the sheet to show her who it is, waves to the audience, then drops the sheet back into place. He moves behind Fusspot and taps him on the shoulder

Fusspot looks round and sees him, screams and exits rapidly, chased by Tickles

The others stop singing

Queen (*grabbing the King's arm*) Cedric. Cedric.

King (*nervously*) It's all right, dear. It's all right. Don't panic. We probably aren't singing loud enough. (*To the audience*) And you were a fat lot of help. You were supposed to be warning us and you never made a sound. I've a good mind to shorten the school holidays for that.

Dame Never mind. Never mind. They'll warn us next time. (*To the audience*) Won't you? (*To the King and Queen*) Let's go on with the singing.

They sing again

Tickles comes back on. This time he moves behind the Queen

King Wait. Wait. Everybody stop singing.

They all stop

They're saying the ghost is right behind us. We'd better have a look.

Tickles bobs down. All turn and look over his head, see nothing, then face front again. Tickles stands

Dame Nobody there. They must be pulling our legs. On with the singing.

They start again. Tickles taps the Queen on the shoulder

  She looks round, sees him, screams and dashes off chased by Tickles

The King and Dame stop singing

King (*trembling*) Semmi? Semmi. Come back. Oh dear. She's gone too. Whatever are we going to do?
Dame Sing louder.

They begin singing again

  A Ghost enters and taps the King on the shoulder. He looks round, sees him, screams and dashes off chased by the Ghost

The Dame folds over with laughter

  I bet they're halfway back to the palace by now. (*She flings her arms round the Ghost*) Oh, Tickles. I've never seen anything so funny in my life. The look on their faces.

They both shake with laughter

  Tickles enters, holding his sheet and laughing

Tickles Here, Ammonia. What did you think to that stroke of genius, eh? (*He stops dead in his tracks as he sees them*)
Dame Tickles? (*She pulls herself free of the Ghost*) Then who's *this*?

The Ghost raises its arms and shrieks with laughter

  The Dame and Tickles yell with fright and exit chased by the Ghost. The cottage door opens and Carabosse appears. She drags the Princess behind her

Carabosse My plans are made. By magic I'll transform your shape and so
    In seconds you'll become, my dear, a timid, snow-white doe.
    Then through these woods, by huntsmen chased, on cloven hoofs you'll fly
    Until exhausted, dazed and torn, your heart is pierced and thus you *die.*
Princess (*struggling*) No. No.

  Azuriel enters R

Azuriel One final chance I give you, Carabosse, to halt your plan.
Carabosse (*scornfully*) You can't harm me, Azuriel.
Azuriel I know. But young Prince Valiant can.
    And lest you free the princess now, an end to you he'll make.
    So come. Admit you're beaten.

Carabosse   No. My chance with him, I'll take.
Azuriel   (*sadly*) Then fare-you-well, dear sister. (*She raises her voice*)
                  Prince Valiant now appear, to fight your greatest battle.
Carabosse   (*looking round*) Yes. Where are you?

The Prince appears from behind the cottage, dressed in shining armour, his sword in his hand

Prince I'm right here.
Princess (*joyfully*) Valiant.

Carabosse flings the Princess aside

Carabosse   (*raising her stick like a sword*) Not even mighty Arthur's
                    sword
                  Will foil my vengeful aim.
                  One touch of *this* means death to you,
                  And *I* shall win the game.
Prince Don't be too sure.

They circle each other cautiously, then Carabosse lunges. Valiant leaps back and counters. A great fight begins

The other principals enter and stand watching, calling encouragement

Finally, Valiant drives Carabosse upstage and thrusts his sword into her. With a great shriek she dies. All cheer. The Princess runs to Valiant and embraces him.

Azuriel   (*stepping forward*) Thus ends the life of Carabosse
                  So from this moment on,
                  All traces of her evil power
                  Will fade, and soon be gone
                  Now to the palace let's return,
                  For 'tis my pleasant duty
                  To prepare it for the wedding day
                  Of Valiant and his Sleeping Beauty.

Everyone cheers loudly and the Lights fade on a scene of general rejoicing

SCENE 6

A corridor in the palace

Shout and Bawl entertain. Tickles may join in

SCENE 7

The great ballroom and Finale

The Lights come up on the Choristers performing a lively dance

Dance (Choristers)

When the dance ends, all exit L and R. The Finale walk-down now begins

Babes
Junior Chorus
Senior Chorus
Fusspot
Shout and Bawl
Azuriel and Carabosse
King Cedric and Queen Semolina
Dame Goodbody and Tickles
Prince Valiant and Princess Aurora

Prince	Our fairy tale is over. Its merry course is run.
Princess	We hope you liked our story, and you've had a bit of fun.
Dame	You've been a super audience. You've filled us with delight
Tickles	So thank you for supporting us. Good luck. God bless. Good-night.

Everyone joins in the final song

Finale

Curtain

FURNITURE AND PROPERTY LIST

PROLOGUE

On stage: Nil

Personal: **Azuriel:** wand (used throughout)
Fairies: wands (used throughout)

ACT I

SCENE 1

On stage: Cut-out windows
Dais. *On it:* two thrones. *To* R: royal cradle
Tables
Balloons, flags, streamer decorations etc.

Off stage: Huge dishes of food etc. **(Servants)**
Large slice of bread **(Tickles)**
Baby wrapped in white lace shawl **(Dame)**

Personal: **Fusspot:** rod of office (used throughout), £5 note in pocket
King and Queen: crowns (worn throughout)
Carabosse: crooked stick (used throughout)

SCENE 2

On stage: Nil

Off stage: Rolled scroll **(Fusspot)**
Paper bag containing a doughnut and jam tart **(Shout)**

Personal: **Bawl:** ten p and three £1 coins in pocket

SCENE 3

On stage: Trees, shrubs etc.
Large garden seat up L

Off stage: Goblet on a small tray **(Fusspot)**

Personal: **Tickle:** ring in small box

SCENE 4

On stage: Nil

SCENE 5

On stage: Cut-out windows
              Dais. *On it:* two thrones
              Tables
              Balloons, flags, streamers etc.

Off stage: Small spinning wheel, stool **(Rats)**
              Silk-covered bier **(Servants)**
              Rose briars **(Stage Management)**

Personal: **Queen:** handkerchief

ACT II

SCENE 1

On stage: Cottage up L with practical door
              Shops and cottages

Off stage: Notice reading: "WANTED—PRINCE VALIANT. APPLY WITHIN"
              (Dame)

Personal: **Prince:** coin in waist pouch

SCENE 2

On stage: Nil

Off stage: Large sword **(Stage Management)**

SCENE 3

On stage: Cut-out windows. *Outside:* rose briars
              Dais. *On it:* two thrones
              Tables
              Balloons, ragged flags and streamers etc.
              Silk-covered bier. *Behind it:* large snake
              NB. all items covered in cobwebs

Personal: **Prince:** sword in scabbard

SCENE 4

On stage: Nil

SCENE 5

On stage: Cottage with practical door

Personal: **Tickles:** white sheet

SCENE 6

On stage: Nil

SCENE 7

On stage: As ACT I, SCENE 5

LIGHTING PLOT

Property fittings required: nil

Various interior and exterior settings

PROLOGUE

To open: pale, pastel lighting

Cue 1	**Azuriel** waves her wand. There is a flash	(Page 1)
	Black-out	

ACT I, SCENE 1

To open: Full, general lighting

No cues

ACT I, SCENE 2

To open: General lighting

No cues

ACT I, SCENE 3

To open: Bright sunshine

Cue 2	**Carabosse** appears L	(Page 18)
	Dim lighting and bring up green follow spot on **Carabosse**	
Cue 3	**Carabosse** exits L	(Page 19)
	Snap off green spot	
Cue 4	**Azuriel** waves her wand and exits R	(Page 19)
	Return to bright sunshine effect	
Cue 5	**Princess:** ". . . if only for a few minutes."	(Page 20)
	Lights flicker	
Cue 6	At the end of Song 5	(Page 25)
	Black-out	

ACT I, SCENE 4

To open: General lighting

Cue 7	At the end of Song 6	(Page 27)
	Black-out	

ACT I, Scene 5

To open: Bright, evening interior effect

Cue 8	**Carabosse** enters down L *Gradual fade to green spot on* **Carabosse**	(Page 31)
Cue 9	**Carabosse** exits L *Return to bright evening interior effect*	(Page 32)

ACT II, Scene 1

To open: Bright sunshine effect

Cue 10	With much excitement they all exit *Quick fade to Black-out*	(Page 40)

ACT II, Scene 2

To open: Dim forest lighting

Cue 11	**Prince** hurries off R *Quick fade to Black-out*	(Page 43)

ACT II, Scene 3

To open: Dim lighting

Cue 12	The rose briars fall from windows *Increase to bright daylight*	(Page 45)
Cue 13	The **Chorus** are very upset, general despair *Black-out*	(Page 49)

ACT II, Scene 4

To open: General lighting

Cue 14	At the end of Song 13 they exit quickly *Black-out*	(Page 51)

ACT II, Scene 5

To open: Gloomy, shadowy lighting

Cue 15	Everyone cheers loudly *Fade to Black-out*	(Page 56)

ACT II, Scene 6

To open: General lighting

No cues

ACT II, Scene 7

To open: Full, general lighting

No cues

EFFECTS PLOT

PROLOGUE

Cue 1	When ready *Flash*	(Page 1)
Cue 2	**Azuriel** waves her wand *Flash*	(Page 1)

ACT I

Cue 3	**Azuriel:** "The gift of——" *Flash*	(Page 10)
Cue 4	**Carabosse:** ". . . our paths have to cross." *Flash*	(Page 11)
Cue 5	At the end of the ballet the **Insects** exit silently *Flash*	(Page 18)
Cue 6	Lights flicker *Flash*	(Page 20)
Cue 7	**Carabosse** casts a spell *Flash*	(Page 31)

ACT II

Cue 8	The **Prince** stoops to kiss **Aurora** *Loud hissing noise behind bier*	(Page 44)
Cue 9	The **Prince** hurries out R *Flash*	(Page 48)

MADE AND PRINTED IN GREAT BRITAIN BY
LATIMER TREND & COMPANY LTD PLYMOUTH

MADE IN ENGLAND